Ageless

5 Keys to a Miraculous Life at Any Age

by
Hedda Adler

TO Julie
may you have a
ageless, happy, miraculous
live ♡

Love
Hedda

10-10-10 Publishing
Markham, ON
Canada

2-22-17

AGELESS
5 Keys to a Miraculous Life at Any Age
www.AgelesstheBook.com
Copyright © 2017 by Hedda Adler

Publisher
10-10-10 Publishing
Markham, ON
Canada
Printed in the United States of America
Title ID: 6868708
ISBN-13: 978-1542603584

Cover design and inside text design/layout by Richard Quinn (415) 531-8404

Cover photo by Richard Quinn ©2016

Dedicated to:

Colette, my beautiful daughter inside and out, you are a beam of light, strength, and love in my life. I feel so blessed to be your mother and so proud of your dedication raising my grandchildren. They are the loving, caring, reflections of you.

Nina, my amazing granddaughter. I am proud, watching you as you conquer the world with your intelligence and beauty. Nothing can stop you from reaching your highest dreams.

Julian, I see a great leader in you, with a beautiful, compassionate heart, guiding many people to happier and more productive lives. The world needs you. I am so proud of you. You have positioned yourself for an extraordinary and fulfilling life.

Philipp, you are so smart and witty. You will be wonderful, helping people stay healthy, with strong visions for their lives. I see you becoming the most loved doctor you dream to be.

Richard Quinn, with love and deep gratitude for your tireless guidance and devotion as my developmental editor, researcher, designer and media producer.

CONTENTS

ACKNOWLEDGEMENTS

My thanks to:

My publisher, Raymond Aaron, for the inspiration to write my book and the truly happy guidance at every step to finish it. My creative editor and designer, Richard Quinn, for the insightful contributions to content and look of this book. My book architect, Cara Witvoet, for the guidance in getting it done on time.
Cheri Jaques, for the amazing editing and long friendship.
Joan Kasich, for the encouragement, inspiration, tireless support and friendship..
Dr. Jean Houston, for the wisdom and encouragement to join with the women of all ages and bring heaven to earth.
Thomas Huebl, for the compassionate wisdom and his sparkling presence.
Miranda MacPherson, for the seeing of my soul and the compassionate welcome to relax my ego and trust the beautiful realms of Grace.
Kimi Avary, for the skillful, insightful and inspired support of my mind, my heart and my spirit.
Jessica Hadari, for the Fem TALKS community and the enthusiasm, joyful commitment and friendship.
Sahar Nafal, for the Bright Side of Life community, the inspiration to accept playing a bigger game and the deep friendship of soul sister.
Gitta Sivander, for the friendship and help to speak with confidence and grace.

Jill Lublin, for the friendship, branding support and many meaningful conversations.

Eileen McKusick, for the pioneering work on the human biofield, her friendship and for tuning my biofield.

Sergio Baroni, for the uplifting consultations, wisdom in all things regarding self-love and the Italian love songs spontaneously erupting during our many dinners.

Marci Shimoff, for the friendship and inspiration to serve others with passionate commitment and to value the wisdom of having great coaches.

Ashanna Solaris, for breathing life into my heart and wardrobe.

Anne Bernard, for the lessons to think big and getting me to go to Australia for my "Date with Destiny."

Tony Robbins, for the guidance and embodied inspiration,

Jackie Forester, for accounting support and friendship.

Ajaya Sommers, for embodying the wisdom of living with direct access with the intelligence of life.

Alessia and Kane Minkus, for the energy, humor and wisdom you generously share in turning mortals into business rockstars

Rebecca Hall Gruyter, for the support and for creating Your Purpose Driven Practice community.

Dr. De Leon, for the 30 long years of watching over my health and refusing to give me drugs.

Terry Thompson, for always standing by my side and sharing your experience and wisdom so generously.

Marilyn Suey, for the financial consulting, gracious introductions and expert advice.

My family, Colette Roemer, for the gift of a loving daughter, filling my heart with pride and enriching my life with 3 incredible grandchildren. Nina Paetau, for the privilege to be her grandmother, Julian and Philipp Roemer, for the honor of having such wonderful grandsons,

The Folmer family, for the joy and goodness added to my life.

Dee Thompson, for the caring friendship.

Carolyn Bournes, for friendship support and the wisdom of health for my body and my heart,

Ines O'Donovan, for creating the Jeunessima Club, the friendship and vision to bring anti-aging to the world.

Neal Rogin, for the laughter that hurts my sides and being a true friend.

Tina Malia, for the gifted voice and inspired music that enchants my heart and lifts it into heaven.

Gary Malkin, for the timeless music, musical direction and supportive friendship.

Alicia Dattner, for the ever vibrant comedy and friendship.

Lloyd Barde And Debra Wilder, for their friendship and uplifting productions.

Cindy Schellenberg, "my Wichtel in Bavaria," for teaching me to see with my heart.

Matt Khan and Julie Dittmar, for making enlightenment feel like a journey home to the family you always knew was there for you.

Lili Bates, for the inspiration to connect the dots between my heart, my health and vitamins.

Diane Weber Shapiro, for the friendship, generous hospitality and enchanted concerts.

Soraya Dadsetan, for the transition into the magnificent culture in Iran and the encouragement to move to California.

Michael Fitzpatrick, for the opening of your heart and cello to the universe of beauty, wonder and breathtaking virtuosity.

Jan Jorgensen Circone, for the luminous and light-hearted friendship.

Jordina Salabert, for the friendship, hospitality, inspiration and courage to speak out on issues that matter.

Sayra Flores, for being my first friend in the US and supporting my personal growth.

Kynthia, for the inspirations, encouragement and friendship.

Dr. Herb Akers and family, for the healing, generosity, hospitality and wisdom that astounded me on many occasions.

Antje and Brody Boyd, for the friendship and generous guidance in matters of love.

Guya Aliquo, for the endless support and friendship.

Peter and Judy Giddings, for the hospitality and for racing vintage cars all over the world in your 70's.

The Danville Chamber of Commerce, for the great support.

Dr. Juris Bunkis, for the friendship and many years of professional support.

Patty Riley, for the friendship, the tenacity of your support and the education concerning my rights.

Robin McDonald, for the friendship and support.

Dr. Chau Phan, for the support and magic of your chemistry.

Diana Rogin, for the joyful friendship and rock solid support.

Helga Kanzler, for keeping my European roots alive in America and reminding me of the kind of friendships that are possible in this world.

Muriel Boyd, for your financial advice and friendship.

Celestino Medina, for enriching the Bemer family with your inspiring insights and kind presence.

Gabriel Zahir Frith, for the joy of witnessing a young, artistic genius in the making.

Berna Garduno, for the support and friendship that thrives over the years.

Linda Mannina and Nancy Gibbons, for their lasting friendship, loyal patronage and many joyful times.

Alexandra Joy Smith, for the family support and coaching inspiration.

Eden Amadora, for bringing to women the rituals of awakening their archetypal powers.

Vishen Lakhiani, for the inspiration to be extraordinary.

Dr. Larry Dossey, for pioneering so many changes in medicine and holding the vision of the Immortality of the Soul.

Kristen Eykel, for her friendship and work to support conscious birthing and empowered living.

Zaya and Maurizio Benazzo, for creating the extraordinary Science and Non-Duality Conference and Community.

The Whole Foods Team, West Berkeley, for making shopping for good food a delightful experience.

*"The life I see Hedda Adler living is an inspiration
to so many women. She has nourished an abundance of
friendships ever since she divorced and left behind the isolation
and invisibility that she suffered through not so long ago. A
new woman has taken shape in the years I have known her.
This woman is far from isolated and has travelled the world to
study with many of the world's greatest teachers and coaches.*

*Hedda has woven a network of dynamic women and
men around her mission to support people to become
independent creators of their lives. No longer invisible and
unappreciated, Hedda has transformed her life and activated
her magnetic love in the service of others.*

*I see many women attracted to her and for good
reason. She radiates the beauty and vitality of a woman thirty
years younger. It is still rare that a woman who has already had
a richly successful career takes up a whole new career as an
author and speaker. To anyone who knows or is blessed to read
Hedda's work will be inspired, motivated and know how to stay
forever young."*

~ JIll Lublin, international
speaker, master publicity consultant and
four times best-selling author -including
Profit of Kindness.

*"I see many powerful women in my events. Few stand
out with the grace, strength and beauty that Hedda Adler does.
She seems to shine with some hidden power that is the
birthright of all women. She is a mother, a grandmother, a*

sincere seeker of truth and wisdom, a world traveller and a successful award-winning aesthetician. I have worked with her and highly recommend her.

I always leave her office looking and feeling ten years younger. I am thrilled that her life and her important message of independence is finding it's way to larger audiences. I know the impact one woman can have and I am thrilled to witness the transformation of Hedda Adler into a change agent and a woman of influence."

~ Jessica Hadari - founder and director
of Fem Talks

"Receiving a face treatment from Hedda Adler is like being blessed in heaven. Hedda is the most thorough facial expert I have encountered in my 25 years of going for treatments all over the world. She uses every minute to give attention to what your skin needs, while also wholeheartedly attending to you as a whole being. I always leave Hedda's office feeling recharged, uplifted and energized. If I were to live out of state, I would fly in to come and get a treatment from Hedda!"

~ Gitta Sivander, dynamic
presentation coach,   Industry Rockstar

"It's not often that I meet someone who, after a short time, I know will be in my life forever. My name is Sahar

Nafal, the founder of The Bright Side of Life Women's Community in the San Francisco Bay Area. A few years ago I had the honor of meeting Hedda Adler. Hedda is a beautiful women inside and out. I am honored to call her a dear friend. She is someone who you want to know. Hedda is a vision of agelessness. I have witnessed firsthand the surprising resilience and abilities she possesses to inspire others to trust themselves to heal, to learn, to transform, to lead and step into their greatness. She applies the same practices to herself.

Hedda is a beautiful being who has a sincere appreciation and love for everyone she meets, wherever she goes. Her reputation is impeccable and she cares deeply for both the women and men who work with her. She inspires us all. Hedda is a radiant example of one who is living agelessly, and thriving in a new culture of human greatness.

Thank you for all you do Hedda."

~ Sahar Nafal, Community
Builder Expert

"Hedda Adler is one of the foremost aestheticians in the country. I have been going to her for over 25 years for my skin care treatments and she has been instrumental in keeping my skin looking radiant and young. Her knowledge, her techniques, her products and her passion about skincare and anti-aging is unsurpassed!"

~ Freddi Wilkenson

"If you haven't had a facial with Hedda Adler, you have no idea what your skin can truly look like. I feel that I'm a good judge of technique since I am a trained Aesthetician myself. I know what it takes to insure the skin is relaxed and open to transformation. Hedda's many years of international training and her compassion are certainly evident when she welcomes you into her world of health and beauty. If you would like to feel rejuvenated from the inside out and feel absolutely gorgeous, I recommend making an appointment soon."

~ Linda Mannina - *Creating Order Out of Chaos*

Hedda Adler

FOREWORD

Every once in awhile I find an idea that needs to be brought to life and someone who can bring it into focus. It has been said that there is nothing more powerful than an idea whose time has arrived. Hedda Adler is leading a new generation of adventurous women and men who are living longer and are committed to creating and living new lives that break free of the cultural "aging" beliefs. Ageless living is an idea and an invitation for you to pursue. This visionary idea is sweeping away ingrained patterns of thought that have held millions of you in a trance of dependency and compliance. A new vision of creating meaning and value during the longer life you will be living is needed. As Einstein is reported to have said in the last century, "There are two ways to live. You can live as if nothing is a miracle or you can live as if everything is a Miracle."

The transforming idea of ageless living, whose time has finally arrived, has been eloquently stated and explored by Hedda. It may be the key for you to actually creating and sustaining a life of miracles. For most of her extraordinary life, Hedda operated a successful skin care business. Her international training and 40 years of practice gives her a unique perspective on the issues concerning aging and maturing. She is the embodiment of this new idea and inspires you to leave behind a world shrouded in the shadows of debilitating beliefs. Ageless Living is a vital reversal of the idea that you, as a human being, inevitably decline after "midlife" and proceed to increase that decline until you die. This is a wake up call - summoning you from the hypnotic slumber of your materialistic cultural beliefs. These beliefs have been shaken for decades by the new breakthroughs in physics, biology, neuroscience, and computer technologies.

Hedda has chosen to dislodge the demeaning labels, restore the hope and clarify the confusing and interwoven beliefs that are holding you imprisoned in living out the cultural "aging commands." Aging is overturned and replaced with a vision of Ageless Living. Maturing free of the aging stereotypes is the adventure Hedda is calling you to. Whether you are young or old, this work will give you the insights and tools to support this idea whose time has come in your own life.

Moving swiftly out of her own slumber in a dysfunctional marriage and lifestyle, Hedda sweeps you along on a voyage of discovery. Waking her up and creating a life free of cultural constraints, Hedda recovered her health, her joy, her courage, and her rights and entered a new world. The new world, transformed by a series of events that, one by one, opened doors into possibilities and potentials that she was completely unaware of before.

Quickened and energized, Hedda's new lifestyle unlocked powers of restoration so deep that her own physical appearance shifted to that of a woman 20 to 30 years younger. Her energy radiates now in a way that strangers stop her in the street wanting to know who she is and what she is doing. This inspiring book came into being as her response to the many requests from her clients and friends stunned by these changes in her, who wanted her secrets.

Ageless living will challenge you, inspire you, guide you and plant in your imagination a vision of how to enjoy the longer life you are blessed to have. Vibrant and ageless living is the way of life that shines within the pages of this book. If you want to live joyfully and realize the miracle of your life, this book is for you. I am so happy Hedda has brought her ideas to the world. The universe needs this new voice of Hedda's to enliven the world and shape a new culture - a culture of Ageless Living.

RAYMOND AARON

New York Times Top Ten Bestselling Author

INTRODUCTION

My goal is to invite you enjoy your long life, examine and rewrite your beliefs about aging. I want you to examine centuries old conditioning, cultural dictates and rules of behavior that have shaped the landscape of your understanding of human aging.

I believe you have a new kind of choice in front of you as you move through time and space. You may either comply to how you "should" biologically respond to the passing of time, obeying the dictates of aging as defined by our current culture or you can choose to shift your focus and occupy your body/mind space with ever increasing worthiness, richness and passion. Here you can embody your own response to a self-actualized life that is vibrantly independent. I view this choice as a powerful tool that frees you to create and enjoy a new kind of culture, with new arts, beliefs, customs and institutions. An ageless living culture will integrate your journey from childhood, youth, adulthood through old age, becoming a seamless adventure of ever increasing competence and value.

Awakening your ageless nature is an emerging technology that is rewriting the cultural behavior codes that have kept billions of human beings in a trance of heedless compliance. Behavior codes are embedded in our culture and embedded inside your body and mind. Ageless living is reshaping the social perception of reality itself, which is the core ordering function of human culture. We agree to agree on the "way things are." This new rewriting of the *human operating system* is creating a new "reality" inside a holistic approach to health. This approach is rooted in the ancient idea that healing is most effective when the whole person is considered, rather than focusing on specific body parts, illnesses, or symptoms. As Socrates stated in the 4th century B.C., "the part can never be well unless the whole is well." In it mind and body are not separate and even the assumption that the mind is in the brain is overwritten with a new code that operates in a radically different worldview. It is far from the worldview of previous generations.

Inside this holistic reality, the new code is being composed and tested in research laboratories, universities, companies, sports centers, large and small learning groups and individuals. Not only are the lifespans of human beings are being lengthened, but the quality of life is being re-coded with new values and new beliefs. These point towards a new vision of life on earth in which humans are thriving in longer and longer lifespans. This book touches on some of these new "codes" and I encourage you to use them to experiment with yourself. Code a new reality, write a unique command sequence that will unlock your unique potential. Erase and write over dysfunctional habits that perhaps have long held you in place.

In the following chapters you will learn how to enjoy living the longer lives we are able to live today. I will share with you my story of overcoming the spell of complying with the cultural conditioning I was exposed to in my home country of Germany. I explore many of the cultural programs we are up against as we shake off limiting beliefs and constricting habits of thought. Important areas in learning to enjoy your long life are; the medicine of the future, the impact of the coming ageless revolution and understanding how valuable and joyful it can be to learn and evolve in groups.

Creating new stories of your self-worth will be explored. My skin care chapter will provide some useful insights for you into this vital area of self-care. You have always been a creative being. Now with the world's knowledge at your fingertips you are more powerful than at any time in modern history. This power can be focused and directed to living long and living well. It is my hope that this book inspire and uplift you to design and live your life in new transforming ways.

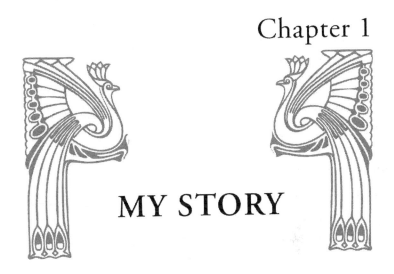

Chapter 1

MY STORY

The five keys to living a miraculous life at any age are five insights. They are insights seen and understood by your mind's eye. They have always been with you. To recover them, activate them and share them will open to you the possibility to live an ageless life from now on. Faster and more effectively than you may be able to comprehend now, your body, mind and spirit can restore your health, energy and creativity. The first of these is to remember that you are the master your life.

I was 12 years old when I told my first lie. Having never lied before, I was nervous about how that would go. I was in Germany, standing in a pharmacy. After working up my courage I said to the pharmacist in my bravest voice, "My mom has a horrible headache and can't get out of her bed. She sent me to get some pills that could help her. Can you help me?" I was holding my breath and gave her my most innocent look. "She should take 4 at a time with lots of water" she instructed and handed me the package with sixty pills. I had been working on my plan for some time and was relieved that this step went so smoothly. I could not confide in anyone nor get anyone's advice. I was on my own and determined to carry out my plan and secure my escape. I walked away knowing she would not assume that it had just taken all my courage to lie to her.

At that time I felt that I was an unloved, useless and ugly first daughter who saw nothing in the days ahead but more yelling at me, more criticism of me. I was experiencing a life of no love, care or emotional support whatsoever. Every time now as my mom started yelling at me I learned to close my ears and whisper to myself "I am a princess, I am a princess, I AM A PRINCESS" and fled to my room. Often times she yelled "Who do you think you are? You are nothing special, you are just an ordinary girl and you have to participate in cleaning and gardening as much as all of us." I knew that, but I didn't like to get my hands dirty, I didn't like to weed in the garden, I couldn't care less to have a self knitted pullover. I preferred to have none, than to wear one I didn't look pretty in. I never received a hug from my Mom, never a word of praise, never an "I love you" no matter what I did to try to please her. The endless frustration of failing to do anything right for her had crushed my spirit.

My little sister, Ingelore, was the apple of her eyes. She was frail and got sick often, which worried mom a lot. Every childhood disease took her twice as long as me to recover from. Mom believed this was due to her nine months of nursing me, even when she wasn't nourished as she should have been. This was right after the war and times were still difficult. She couldn't nurse Ingelore for more than a few months. My sister bit her nipples so badly that she got a painful infection and needed to feed her formula. I saw that the love I so needed was always shown toward my sister. I could see it there in front of me. I could see it at school with the other children and their mothers. I could see it was possible. Possible for others, but not for me. Not ever for me no matter what I did. I simply could not bear the agony of that loveless life another day.

Dad was always working, leaving in the morning before we woke up and coming home late after 9:00 or 10:00pm. Night after night, before he came completely through the door, my mom started to complain about our fighting and how awful I was to annoy her so much. One night was particularly telling. During the afternoon Ingelore had ripped my only doll's legs out and when I slapped her hands she screamed bloody murder that resulted in my Mom running towards me and hitting my head so hard that I saw stars flying through it. Her horrible loud yelling about how disgusting I was, paralyzed my heart and stunned my mind. I was given no opportunity to explain what triggered me to slap her hands. Ingelore enjoyed watching me being punished like that and gave me the smirky smile which often would follow such times. This devastated me beyond imagination. I couldn't take it anymore.

I was so sad. I dreamed up a woman who would like to adopt me. I longed so deeply for a mom who would want me, hug me, encourage me, laugh with me and like me just the way I was. Most of all I yearned for her to tell me that she is proud of me and my accomplishments in school. I worked so hard believing this might bring the love I desperately wanted. If any woman would have offered her hand and said to me on the street "Would you like to come with me and be my daughter?" I would not have hesitated for a moment; I would happily have gone with her, never to return home.

My secret plan to get the pills I needed worked. Finally I would be able to fall asleep and never wake up here again. I could be free.

I left the Pharmacy and walked to the nearby forest that was not too far from our home. It started to rain and I was huddling next to a giant chestnut tree imagining what would happen next. Would I have excruciating pain? Would I just easily fall asleep? Would my family miss me? How would Dad react? I felt bad to hurt him but, on the other hand, I couldn't handle for even one more single time to be exposed to my mother disliking me so much. I opened the bottle and started to swallow one pill after another until they were gone without any water. I was nauseated and the rain started to pour so hard that a little stream began to flow right in my direction. Soaking wet and cold I soon fell asleep. I can't recall for how many hours I was sitting there drenched in water. I was in a fog. Nothing felt real to me. I started moving towards my home. My parents were always deep sleepers and I managed to quietly sneak into my bed after drying myself with a towel and hiding my drenched clothes under the bed.

Suddenly I felt cold again. My bedcovers were ripped off me, and my Mom was yelling at me. "You are late for school. You are such a lazy little girl. Get up right now.

Up!" All I could think was "She is here in Heaven also?" I was devastated. I could not bear that thought.
She literally whipped me out the door despite my pleas that I was not feeling well and was so ill. I didn't want to face the fact that she was here, still around me. The moment I arrived in class, I apologized for being late and sat down. I was so ill, I can still recall the magnitude of my sickness to this day. After two hours observing my pale face and my holding of my hurting belly my teacher sent me home.

I did not recover quickly and 4 days later I collapsed in the bathroom. Our doctor came and ordered me to stay in bed for the next two days. After returning to school my home life continued to be unchanged and I endured my situation thinking mostly of how fast I could leave and be on my own. My joy where the projects in my art classes. I had a passion for sculpting, I had fleeting moments of accomplishments in seeing my creations come to life. I also had a gift for watercolor painting. My artwork was displayed all over the school, which made me very proud. Both of my teachers supported my work and praised my efforts and talents. During those times I felt inspired and distracted from my home life.

One day I discovered a bird's nest hidden deep within a huge hedge next to our house. There were four eggs in it and I started to visit it every day, carefully noting down the developments. I was happy and very protective of my little bird family. I wrote an essay on the nest and the comings and goings of life inside the hedge. My essay won the honor of the highest rated story and everyone in my class applauded me for it. Our school principal, who was also my art teacher, suggested to my parents that they send me to an art school. I was thrilled at the idea. Instead of trusting our principal or having any regard for my feelings they enrolled me in a business administration school. That I should like and select my own profession meant nothing those days. I hated it from the first day till the last day, three and half years later.

One bright light in my early years was my grandmother. It was always a special joy to visit our Omi Anna. She was the embodiment of a loving, caring grandma. We all adored her so much. I was always fascinated to observe her during her evening beauty ritual. It left her with my beloved Omi smell. During one of our visits when I was seven, I was longing to get some of her cream for my own face and I asked "May I use some of your cream Omi?" She paused for a moment; put that magical blue jar of NIVEA cream onto her left palm and said "If you promise me to wash your face every night, so there is no sweat or dust on your face, then I will allow you to use the cream." Her arm reached over and the blue jar was right in front of my face. I felt so honored that she allowed me to use her cream. I would smell like her, I was in heaven. To this day I always have a little jar next to my bed and she magically appears in my memory as soon as I apply some over my lips, and I feel her smiling at me.

If anybody would have told me that Omi Anna had just set my life's path in motion, one that would become my passion and would take me around the world from Europe to Iran and all the way here to California, I would have not believed them. If someone had pointed out that one day I would impact thousands of women, enhancing their beauty and uplifting their self-esteem and confidence, I would have fainted on the spot. A loving seed was planted there in my heart that would touch so many women thanks to my Omi Anna.

Growing up the way I did taught me that living without love and appreciation can be unbearable. I know what that feels like and made up my mind to never miss a day or an opportunity to kiss and hug my own daughter, letting her know how much I love her and how proud I am about her accomplishments. She is the greatest blessing of my lifetime and it is an honor and privilege to be her mother.

She herself became such a loving caring mother, her devotion to her daughter and two sons is so touching for me to observe. I am adoring this beautiful spirit she is, inside and out.

I learned that the loving trust my grandma placed in me at seven had a huge impact on my life. Even so, I don't remember her kissing me or saying that she loved me. She just showed it by the way she honored me with her own precious possession, ready to share. When our visit ended, she called me to her and asked me to close my eyes and hold out both my hands. I felt something cold placed on my hands and when I opened my eyes, there was a small jar of Nivea Cream. Smiling lovingly she said "So now you will be able to continue your beauty ritual at home." With that my life path was carved out.

AGELESS LIVING

I believe Ageless Living is a way of life that has a foundation in courageous trust. Yes, it is joyful, energetic, and positive, but the embracing of life's gifts can also be very painful. These gifts sometimes come wrapped in betrayals, abandonment, times of shame, times of loss and obstacles of all sorts. Meeting all these blocks takes insight and courage. We must have an insight to trust that, hidden in the good and bad is an opportunity, and the courage to move ahead in the face of setbacks and disappointments. Ageless Living is also living free from the cultural beliefs and labels of aging as defined by a materialistic society, whose shallow and flat visions of human life generate an endless flow of destructive aging messages. I was robbed of the qualities of vitality and attractiveness that are, I believe, my birthright when I lived under their spell. These destructive messages became ingrained in my beliefs, my language and my perceptions of reality often for no other reason than that they were just there, everywhere unquestioned by me.

I made up my own mind in response to what I was witnessing. I stopped accepting other people's ideas and challenged the so called "authorities", who are conditioning my mind to accept aging as a slow descent to death, or in extreme conditions had the arrogance to pronounce how long my body was to stay alive. I have heard stories of wonderful, creative individuals who, upon hearing these death sentences responded by saying, "No, I do not accept your story of my future. I will write my own." There are now records of so many people who have challenged the short life spans they were "given" and went on to live long and healthy lives.

These "prognoses" are just stories. The word itself is the fancy, official sounding word to make it easier for you to buy into the "authority" of the person using it. It is from the Greek word *prognōsis*, literally meaning, foreknowledge. I am wary of handing over my right to determine my own "prognosis" to anyone. I am free to accept it and I am free to reject it. We are all free to affirm life, to hold our own beliefs about life and stand in our own authority and sovereignty. We can say how it is going to be for us and create our own prognosis. For the moment my prognosis is to feel exactly as I felt when I was in my thirties and to thrive, having gained the wisdom and insights that are the fruit of many life experiences. These have uncovered my courageous trust in life and in my strength of resolve.

Thousands of women have come to me to look and feel younger, yet so many are repeating the aging conditioning of our society, unaware that they are living out these beliefs and shaping their bodies to conform to values that they do not question. During my 45 years in the Skincare Industry, all too often I have heard statements such as "I am getting old, it's my 50th birthday, just look at me," "I'm too old for this or that" or "What's the point, I just have to accept it's all downhill from here."

They all have one thing in common, they center around aging as a negative stigma, a mental and physical deterioration and reduction of their beings towards a confused and diminished end. I have heard thousands of variations on this theme. This depressing shrinking of vitality and meaning along with a confused outcome is affecting their energy and willingness to even try to change themselves. I have come to see that a big change is needed in our culture if we are to turn around the current aging attitudes and replace them with new beliefs, new thoughts, new actions, habits and values that will give us a new vision of our destiny as human beings. From the moment I was born I have been successful in life and can, if not brainwashed with contrary and degenerating assumptions, stay vibrant and attractive in every moment of my life.

Self-Actualizing Women and Men
Enjoy Taking Risks and Trusting Life

Awakening your ageless nature is saying "Yes" to life itself in all it's beautiful wonderment. It is choosing to live free of any cultural age beliefs that are contrary to the thriving vitality of your body, mind and spirit, day after day, season after season and year after year.

Women question me quite often "How is it Hedda, that you look so much younger than a few years ago when I saw you last?" or "It is amazing that you are not aging. In fact you look like you are aging backwards. What are you doing? How can I learn this?" I would like to see every woman transforming into this joyful state of a new life experience. I am also aware that without the cultivation of a courageous trust in the core of their hearts, the journey toward lasting and ageless vitality will not have a foundation. Missing this foundation myself, I struggled for many years in a loveless childhood, two broken marriages and suffered long-lasting and deep emotional pain.

MY LIFE IN IRAN

I was nineteen when I met the striking Military Attache' of the Iranian Embassy in Cologne, Germany. We fell in love, had a commitment ceremony in Paris and one year later I gave birth to my beautiful daughter Colette in Cologne. The day she finished her first class of elementary school we were called to return to Tehran. Colette flew ahead to Tehran to start her second school year at the German School on time. She was staying with friends who spoke German and that gave the two of us time, to drive from Cologne to Teheran. That marvelous trip was one of the most adventurous times of my life. We started from Cologne, travelled through Austria, Yugoslavia, Bulgaria and on to Istanbul, Turkey. We visited the famous Blue Mosque in Istanbul. Then we spent a few days with friends before we boarded our ship and started through the Black Sea towards the Iranian border where we arrived at the beginning of October 1974. A driver was sent to drive us the remaining hundreds of miles to Teheran. Iran was a magnificent country. We passed through many villages of ancient times. Everything was different and I felt drawn to the adventure, curious about what the next years would have in store us.

Finally we arrived at our destination. Soon we were invited to be the guests of honor at a large welcoming party with over 400 guests near one of the Royal Palaces. A seamstress was hired to design a beautiful dress for me. A driver, servant and a cook were assigned to us. That was the prelude to a life of one thousand and one Arabian Nights. How many hands did I shake that night; two of my sisters-in-law introduced me tirelessly to every single guest. I was welcomed with so much pride. I had just turned twenty-seven that July, I was the young wife of their only brother. It was quite an unexpected, fairytale like experience.

In the midst of the first hour of this lavish party, two twenty foot high doors opened and an old couple stood there waiting to be welcomed. The lady was dressed in a beautiful burgundy dress and her husband in a grey suit with a light blue tie. Silence fell on the hundreds of noisy conversations and from one second to the next you could hear a needle fall. The room was completely and utterly silent. As the couple entered, the guests quickly moved out of their way, stepping aside bowing and holding their hands over their hearts. I was fascinated by the respect that was shown to this mysterious couple. As they walked slowly past us, they both nodded their heads and gave us the most welcoming smile. As they approached their wide couch-like seat they turned around, opened their arms and said simply "Please continue." in Farsi.

Right away the four hundred hundred voices picked up their conversations exactly where they had left off. It was amazing to me. I was so curious and asked my husband "Are they Royals?" and he said "No, they are the parents of the host." I asked again "Is this only happening when guests are visiting?" He said "No, we are honoring our elders who are always our highest priority." I was so impressed. I realized that I liked living in a world where our elders are honored. I felt blessed to witness a society that practiced such way of life. For a brief moment the thought of being respected in in my older days showered me with a wave of a loving sensation and I felt at home right away. How little did I know about the respectful way the Iranian people honor and respect their elders. The following years I immersed myself in that beautiful culture, which I will always cherish in my heart and soul.

Soon an invitation to join the Royal Family for a banquet was delivered to us and my life in Iranian High Society began and was to last for three magical years. When I was young I loved to read the fairy tales about Kings and Queens and followed the news of the modern day Royal families around the world. How could I have ever imagined that I would be actually living inside a Royal Court? I was an ordinary girl from a small town in Germany who ended up winning the heart of the Queen Mother of Iran. She granted me the privilege of sharing her Majesty's presence at any time in her Royal Palace. Many days and nights I participated in the activities of one of the last powerful Monarchies on earth. I am thankful that even to this day the memories of those dramatic and enchanted times are a reminder of life's wisdom and wonderment.

I share more about my training in Europe and my life in America, as well as more stories from my early years in post-war Germany, in Chapter 9.

Chapter 2

AWAKENING MY AGELESS NATURE

There were four key turning points on my own rocky path of awakening my ageless nature. I experienced them at four different stages in my life. The first was the point at which the power of my autonomy emerged, the second was the acceptance of spiritual help, the third was the point at which my self-worth was strong enough to support my standing up for my right to grow and thrive. The fourth turning point was feeling a powerful bond with women who have been persecuted and whose right to life itself was denied through history. I came to finally see clearly the power of my own rights, my need to claim and defend them, and stand heart and soul, united with the many women who are heroically doing the same.

AUTONOMY

The first turning point occurred when I was still quite young. At the age of 10, the subject of dying came up one day in the classroom at my school in the small town of Hameln, Germany. I can still remember, quite vividly, my feelings and the conviction that stirred in me. I was startled, to say the least, at what was being presented to my class and I refused to let fear of the unknown take hold of me. I looked around the classroom and thought to myself, "I am made out of a different material - I will never die!" And that was "it" for me! I never looked back.

Little did I realize, that this conviction was an early manifestation of my autonomy, my ability to decide for myself what is true for me. Nor could I or my teacher and classmates realize how limited these lessons were with regards to the actual nature of our miraculous bodies. The next 50 years, however, would prove to upset almost all the long held understandings of matter, energy and life itself. Indeed, I actually was made of a material far different from the biological thinking of the 1950's. These discoveries would proceed to radically transform not only biology, but medicine and psychology.

SPIRITUAL HELP

The second turning point came 30 years later when I had a close call with death. In the midst of a highway accident I felt as if hundreds of invisible hands held and protected me from an unthinkable calamity not only for me but many surrounding people in their vehicles. I was driving on a rainy day and my car hit a pool of water. I hydroplaned all the way from the left side of the freeway over to the very far right lane crashing into a wall. A huge, fully-loaded Chevron gasoline truck couldn't stop in time and ripped the rear of my car apart. It was the first rain of the year on that Saturday, the police were overwhelmed, attending to 68 crashes happening within an hour around the Bay Area. Only a fire truck could be sent to to secure the scene of my accident. The firefighters checked me out and guided me to their truck helping me to climb up into the cabin for safety.

To this day I can recall the look on one of the fireman's face as he said to me, "You are so lucky - your car is only two inches away from those fuel valves- that truck is fully loaded. If those had broken open this would have been a fiery inferno and you along with at least 30 other cars would have been destroyed in it." When I looked at the scene below me I started to shiver - I was and still am afraid of being around these large tanker trucks. I am always careful and try to pass them to be out of their way as quickly as I can. And yet here I was, after hitting the wall, exactly such a truck crashed into the back of my car because it couldn't stop fast enough. I sensed an unknown sensation in my heart that left me feeling humble and held in a magical embrace.

This was the first time that I had experienced invisible help in such a dramatic way. It would form a foundation for me. I could not see then how much these invisible realms of grace would become part of my life.

Soon after, life returned to normal and my total attention went back to my clients, who needed their time with me for their physical and emotional wellbeing. My skin care practice filled my days with meaningful experiences of rejuvenation and compassion. Helping women have beautiful skin really changed them in deeper ways than simply looking better. They felt different and approached their lives with a renewed confidence.

MIRACULOUS TRANSITION

My life was soon to undergo a third pivotal change that would further support my journey. I have had two marriages and gave birth to one daughter. The first marriage was a world of extreme contrasts in which I was swept up into the Royal Society of Iran. I was confronted with the adventure of a lifetime. On one hand I was welcomed and traveled throughout the length of this magnificent country so rich in spiritual history. On the other hand I tasted the callous disregard for women's rights and faced in my marriage an insurmountable obstacle regarding the expression of my right to grow and develop as I wanted to. It was only through a dramatic intervention that took me to Germany to study before the revolution that I was able to escape the catastrophic persecutions that affected many members of my family. My daughter was safely returned to me in Germany just before the revolution changed the country forever. Her father was denied passage and remained in Iran. Eventually he passed away and I never saw him again.

DISCOVERING MY SELF-WORTH

Years later in the US I married again into a middle eastern family. I thought my new family was more western and modern. It quickly became clear that there would be very little concern about my needs, and that I was expected to totally merge into their traditional Iranian lifestyle. I treasured my Sundays. It was my only time for rejuvenation. I created a beautiful garden which became a sanctuary. Here I would deeply enjoy the peace in my heart and soul; here I could recharge for the coming week. I enjoyed the teachings nature presented to me from the smallest insects to bees, birds, scorpions, black widows, different snakes moving through the grasses and even the tarantulas. I deeply respected and cherished the activities around me. Even the baby canaries landed on my wide brimmed hat on their way to become skilled flyers. By observing and caring for plants, flowers and animals, nature in return taught me to see, feel and understand a world of wonderment which so many don't even know exists.

It is customary in the Iranian culture for family members to visit unannounced. Arriving at any time, I was always expected to immediately drop my activities in my garden or home and join the spontaneous gatherings.

I felt unappreciated, and God forbid if I dared to complain or asked to let me know ahead of time. Month after month and season after season this precious time that I so much needed for my own renewal was taken up in socializing with the extended family. My emptiness and sadness grew. As a result of this, I turned to food and I gained over 20 pounds. As the years went on more and more effort was needed to hide from my clients the sense of how I struggled emotionally. There was nothing to look forward to coming home, other than watching TV. There was never music playing in my house, no stimulating conversations, no birthday celebrations and the wedding anniversaries were completely ignored. I now can see that I betrayed my own self by complying with the family's way of living because my own self-worth was so low.

Over the years, when we still lived in our own house, there was less and less appreciation for my efforts to decorate the house for Christmas and have festive dinners. Often during the holidays I drove myself to our beautifully decorated Village, and stopped in the side streets to catch a little Christmas magic by watching all the happy activities in other people's homes. I missed my daughter's family and grandchildren in Germany. I needed these moments with myself, dwelling on those beautiful memories of the Christmas seasons I grew up with. I embraced these hurting emotions sweeping gently through my soul, re-living my heritage like a movie in those moments alone. After all the years of nobody around me caring, I stopped the decorations and any special Christmas Eve dinners, protecting myself from hurting so much. It actually felt good to cry and I let the tears run to ease my loneliness and pain. To break that cycle, I would start the car, refresh my makeup and said silently to myself, "There will be another Christmas next year and who knows how the world will be then."

I trained myself once again, never to dwell too long in my pain and flicked it off by saying, "It is just an emotion." and went back home. I was OK to finish my Christmas evening like any other by having dinner in front of the television screen. Half of my marriage of almost 30 years existed only on paper. I tried my best to ignore that fact for way too many years. It was only when I was diagnosed with a life threatening health condition that I was forced to understand the urgency to change my life. Now my physical survival was at stake. I took a giant leap of faith and initiated our divorce. We both agreed to part amicably. A new chapter in my life was beginning. In my tender newfound excitement and anxiety I could not have anticipated what was to come from the family I had served and loved for almost 30 years of my life.

We agreed to inform the family by visiting them to announce our divorce and started with my favorite sister-in-law who I love so dearly. She had become like my own sister during those 28 years we spent together. My husband explained to her what a hero he was to so generously set me free, since I aspired to become a coach, traveling around the world. He said, "She will not have time to care for me." Of course the reality was he would never have "set me free." Like so many women today, I was the one who had to bear the burden of initiating the divorce.

I was quiet and just observed my sister-in-law's face which turned into a motionless sculpture. Tears were running down my face as I got up to tell her how sorry I was to bring her this sad news, she shrugged me off and said coldly, "That's ok, I wish you all luck in your life." I was then ushered to the door, no questions asked and I left. Days later I was shocked to my core with the news that she had ordered the entire extended family to never talk to me again. Almost 30 years of devotion and service to my former family ended without so much as a thank you, a chance to plan any path of unity or interaction. Nothing. My eyes were opened to the painful truth of the life I had been living. To this day nothing has changed. Not one of the entire family has found their way to me on their own. I had given all I could to building my life as a loyal member within that family. It was my family and I enjoyed helping out any time there was a need for it. I became a confidant they could trust. The shock of this shattering news affected me so deeply that I was forced to make a clear decision. After getting used to my freedom, I chose to be a "victor and not a victim!" I needed to move forward and let go of my emotional stress. I realized more deeply the gift I had given to myself. I had set myself free.

This is the second key. To remember that I am perfectly made and valuable beyond measure.

The most important task ahead of me now was getting to know myself in new ways and remember how valuable I am. New people came swiftly into my life. The friendships of amazing women who supported and comforted me ignited the warmth and magic of a real and lasting sisterhood and life began anew for me. The discovery of my own potential and the realization of my purpose started blossoming in my work with Dr. Jean Houston and the Austrian spiritual teacher, Thomas Huebl at the Institute for Noetic Sciences (IONS) in Petaluma, California. I gifted myself five days with Tony Robbins on the Gold Coast of Australia. Here I attended his powerful training "A Date with Destiny." As this event unfolded I received his wisdom and felt the support of those attending with me. I was also the recipient of his personal blessing, feeling his huge hand on my head during one of our guided meditations and sensing energy sweeping through my body. A new dimension of being opened in me, and a new understanding about who I am changed my life forever.

> My personal transformation was so profound and powerful that I literally reversed my appearance by 20 years.

I became "mindful" of everything I did. I began eating organic foods, exercised, meditated and left the sugar, bread and carbohydrates out of my diet. I proceeded to lose 25 pounds without even thinking about it. My high frequency energy now radiates in such a positive way that strangers stop me in the streets to talk to me. I used to feel like an "old lady" in my mid 50's. I felt heavy with no energy in my body and with no love and appreciation in my life. Now everything was turning around. How miraculous my new found vision about my myself; the magical change in my appearance, the joyful attitude, the belief in my own strength, the realization of how capable I actually am changed everything I had known about myself. I felt as if wings were growing in my heart and I connected the dots between how and why I selected my new last name "Adler." It means eagle in German. I wanted to soar above all the pettiness I had been enduring, start a new life and help other women break through their confinement. I wanted to see women freed from the limiting circumstances and confining lifestyles that diminish their inherent greatness. Once free, I never looked back, and started to help women joining together to reshape our society the way we would like it to be.

Be yourself AND CHOOSE YOUR OWN BELIEFS IT'S YOUR LIFE!

THE RIGHTS OF WOMEN

On a sunny afternoon in the hills of Northern California a particularly vivid experience unfolded for me quite unexpectedly. Time itself seemed to stop - a spiritual window opened up in the well lit room. This was the second day of a training facilitated by Dr. Jean Houston at the Institute Of Noetic Science. It felt like a gateway was materializing that could carry us to distant times and places. Jean asked us to stand up, giving lots of space to one another and launched into a beautifully spoken meditation. She started by paying tribute to all women, she thanked our mothers for giving us life and invited us to release any lingering pain from our hearts. She then eloquently moved on to our grandmothers and great grandmothers, further and further traveling back through the generations. Each wave of thankfulness wove profound and powerful connections with all the women who walked centuries before us. I could feel my entrance into the different eras, seeing people and even smelling strange and different smells. I saw "witches" with stones around their necks being drowned or tortured to death. I could see people passing swiftly by me. Some of them were looking at me smiling and some were simply curious with no emotions. The intensity of energy heated up as the music accompanying the meditation grew more dramatic. I began shaking and hurting. I was feeling the unimaginable pain they endured, being tortured ever since mankind existed. I literally drowned in my own tears and was riddled with pain.

The journey into those unknown moments in time left me deeply changed and forever curious about that experience. Even now sometimes during my meditations I get flashbacks where, for a brief moment, pictures flash in front of my eyes, but before I am completely aware they are gone. These make me wonder what message the spirits want me to share with the world. The honor to work with Dr. Houston, the heart to heart connection and the gift of enlightenment under her guidance deeply touches and uplifts my heart. The violations of women's rights continues today and I feel it is a huge challenge and honor to play a part in stopping the abuses and directing our vision to a view of the future where women thrive without fear.

EVERYTHING IS AVAILABLE TO YOU.

I am so proud to share that I am 70 now. Most are astounded and speechless when they learn this! Clients and friends asked me to please share with them what it is I do. "We want what you have" they often say. Women and men deeply desire to feel young, energetic and beautiful. The design of my Ageless Living Academy workshops came to life as a result of these many requests.

True beauty starts on the inside and radiates outward. Yes, the nourishment of your amazing temple and how you honor and care for it is essential, it will radiate through you to your skin. Your mental attitude will do the rest. When you research and learn more about the walking miracle you are, when you discover the power and capabilities sleeping within you, you will want to bow in front of your own self. You will never ever feel inadequate, not good enough, not pretty enough or not successful enough ever again.

You are a walking, amazing miracle. You have the power to change your destiny and know that EVERYTHING is AVAILABLE TO YOU.

Trust me, I have experienced it personally and that's why I wrote this book - so that you can be the determined and strong captain of your precious life. Take charge of your own health. Surround yourself with positive people who lift you up. Find your purpose and go on an expedition of discovery about YOU. Follow some simple recommendations on what your body needs and be rewarded by living in a pain-free, energetic and ageless way. There really is no such thing as "old" if you experience the miracle of transformation. It is your mindset that makes all the difference. Let's join together for a revolution. The Revolution of Ageless Living. Staying awake to life with a felt urgency was summed up beautifully by Gandhi when he said,

"Live as if you were to die tomorrow.
Learn as if you were going to live forever."

It is clear that the visions of human life, our meaning, our nature, our origins and destiny are undergoing more changes in less time than at any time in our recorded history. In the last 100 years our understanding of physics and biology have woven together a breathtaking picture of our bodies as vast, interwoven systems of cellular activity, energetic intelligences, molecular responses to emotions and thoughts. Many of the discoveries leading to these new visions still remain outside of the culture of aging because there are so many political, medical, and economic interests that are still running on the older models. In the new science, every human being is seen as profoundly woven into the web of life and has a body of limitless capacity to see, hear, thrive, wonder, dream and be the home of an immortal soul.

No one said to me when I was ten that I have the right to make up my own mind about what my body is, what I am here for or what my end is - if any at all. Like the vast majority of people at this time in history, I was "educated" to accept as true the current models of reality. I am inviting you to wake up to the possibility that we human beings may be much, much more than we are being told. And that as we go deeper as a species and realize our profound interconnectedness with all of life, you may begin to see that you are in a position of expressing the "life principle" itself in a richness that is truly astounding. This life principle, this impulse to live and thrive is what you are. I believe the origin of this life principle is very ancient, that its very nature shimmers with inexhaustible vitality and that the destiny of this living fabric is truly glorious. I do not believe you have to die to get to heaven, that you have to suffer a long painful descent, to fade away in the twilight years or that you have to retire from work you love, only to play golf or sit on a beach getting drunk in a retirement community. No! This is not for me and I know this is not for many of you. You are paving the way for yourself, and many who will follow you, to live vital and meaningful lives without the "prognosis" of inevitable decline, loneliness and irrelevance handed to you by advertising companies, fear mongering medical experts and an endless parade of drug empires. No thank you. You can choose an ageless life that has no "final act" which calls for a curtain to be pulled over your beauty, your wisdom, your vitality or your purpose.

In the next chapter you will learn about changes in science and medicine that are capable of reshaping your understanding of what your body is, and explore practices and technologies that unlock new capacities for your ageless living.

Chapter 3

THE MEDICINE
OF THE FUTURE

Enjoying your long life is going to require the insights, skills and practices to stay healthy for many more decades than any previous generation has enjoyed. Anticipating and planning for longer lives is fast becoming an area of great concern in the fields of health care.

The third key to a miraculous life at any age is remembering to be courageous. The prison of aging beliefs needs to be confronted and understood. It takes courage to look into your heart and mind and see that most of your life may have been spent in confinement. It takes courage to decide to leave behind what is familiar, what is "known." Many changes are needed to live free of societies labels and prescriptions. Most of all, changes in perception and attitudes are required to successfully escape from the dysfunction "aging" beliefs that are embedded in our modern world.

I feel that among the most important of all changes in the last two centuries are the changes in our perceptions and beliefs about the nature of our beautiful human bodies. These changes continue to alter every aspect of our lives. Once our bodies were thought to be the sublime home or temple of the Spirit. This human form has also descended in our views today to be, in some cases, nothing more than a piece of meat struggling to stay alive and breathing in a meaningless universe.

I took a personal journey in an intimate way. I have moved through a maturing vision, a changing perception and a renewed feeling about the inner workings of my unique body.

My relationship with my structure and its rhythms began before I could think, speak, or sense the vast world into which I was moving. It is a journey that began literally inside another human being, my mother. I emerged within a deep connection to the living matrix of another human being. I felt that perhaps this realization could lead me in a new direction of inquiry about the nature of my life. This profound connection and embrace is usually associated with the heart's ability to respond with the appropriate intelligence.

Feeling into the alignment of my senses and my heart, I shifted my questioning from what is possible to what is appropriate. I felt excitement in discovering that I am so much more than I could have imagined a decade ago. Now I was clearly on the path of endless curiosity- to learn, to sense and to experience these expanded ideas about consciousness and how they were affecting my life in so many ways. There was no turning back now. A significant pattern began to emerge for me. The holistic model of health, with its inclusive views that focused on the wellness of life rather than the sick-care views that dominate most of our medical institutions today, was calling me to go deeper.

At the present time holistic research is going ever deeper in its questioning of where our minds actually are located. Our miraculous bodies seem to be able to not only communicate intelligently but generate all manner of organic structures to carry complex information instantaneously to all parts of what Dr. Mae-Wan Ho calls our liquid crystal matrix.

Not so long ago, a friend told me of an unusual Samoan healer who had been trained in both the traditional Samoan healing arts as well as western chiropractic modalities. He had moved from New Zealand to the US and was living in Northern California. My friend had a "miraculous recovery" regaining her ability to walk in only one session with him. Barely able to get out of the car to visit him, she left his office bounding down stairs and briskly walking independently once again. I trusted my intuition and decided I had to see for myself if his reputation was exaggerated or if he did indeed possess a unique synthesis of healing modalities.

I drove the long drive from San Francisco to Sacramento where his office is, hoping I would not be disappointed. After a warm greeting I found myself standing in front of Dr. Herb Akers. He didn't ask any questions and just slowly took me in - from head to foot, scanning my body with his intelligent and curious eyes. He asked me to lie on his table and began to work. So intuitive and fluid was his skill that when the friend who attended the session with me asked, "Would it be alright to ask you a few questions while you work," he smiled and responded that he not only could but would be delighted. I was curious and intrigued, soaking up the wisdom he was sharing, but I was also rather surprised to be subjected to what I later learned was the restructuring of the "memory of my fascia." The fascia was brought to light by the Germans, who pioneered the early research and discovery it's previously unknown functions.

Some of the work he did on my body was light pressure and some was deep and painful, not what I expected. To be honest, I had not experienced such pain since childbirth and was entertaining more than once the thought, "O my God I can't take this!" But such is the Samoan way and such is the treatment style of most practitioners who work in this unique area of changing and erasing muscle memory. I learned much that day about the intelligence in the fascia, how it stores information and embeds it in our musculature and how it can be "erased" and released by restructuring the tissues. The body releases the memories that it thinks are happening in present time and returns to a balanced harmony. To Dr. Akers this balanced harmony restores the body's structure to be and function in perfect health. When, after about 1 hour, he was satisfied with all that could be done that day he said, "Ok, now slowly get up, stand beside the table for a minute and then walk down the halls of my office."

This was the first time in years, ever since my two broken back injuries, that I felt I had my legs back. The feeling I was experiencing had been missing for me for a long, long time. He said, " What had happened was that the injuries caused a detachment from your lower torso and your upper body compromised to take control of your legs, which caused you to feel like a robot, dragging yourself around with your upper body only." Needless to say, I was elated! I felt my body was whole for the first time ever! A new dimension of being, once again, was spread out before me. Since then I have had many long dinners together with his wife and family. I have come to learn that our western approaches to healing are very much in the early stages of profound and far reaching changes in both the understandings of diagnostic approaches and the various treatments being employed. This was another confirmation for me that the holistic model of health was working.

Next on my journey was a scientific shift that ran counter to everything I had be raised to believe. Like many of my generation my attention has been directed to "brain research." New breakthroughs in neuroscience make headlines almost every week and vast amounts of funding and research are centered on the human brain. For years I saw the value and believed the assumption that "cracking the workings of the brain" would unlock the mysteries of human consciousness, that we would finally have at our fingertips the knowledge to improve human life in a myriad of ways. There was one major problem. Research began emerging showing that the brain was not the one command center it was assumed to be after all. It was discovered that the heart is more densely packed with nerve cells and was sending out much more powerful electromagnetic fields of information. I also learned that our bodies are communicating in ways that are completely outside the nervous system. It seems that our nervous system, relying on chemical signaling, is very slow in comparison to the other instantaneous modes, such as electric, electromagnetic and light. These make it possible for our bodies to have holistic communication at the speed of light.

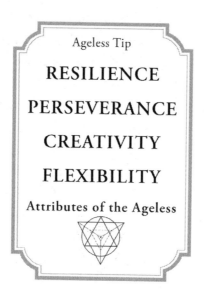

Ageless Tip

RESILIENCE

PERSEVERANCE

CREATIVITY

FLEXIBILITY

Attributes of the Ageless

The new view is that our minds exist throughout our body. That was a big shift from the understanding I grew up believing. However this was followed by an even more challenging view and really pushed my limits. It is the view that my body is "inside" my mind. Here I had come to the big hurdle. I understood that there's no treatment that treats just the mind and that there is no treatment that addresses only the body. I could grasp that they are a unit, working together. But working together is one thing, however the body being literally "inside" the mind is quite another thing.

Some of the findings of Jacob Lieberman, OD.,Ph.D. point to such changes in our current understandings. He wrote:

"So, where's the mind? Not in the head. Not in the body. So, where's the body? The body is inside the mind. It's not the body that creates the mind, as we used to think. It's a mind field of energy, a non localized area of intelligence, that creates what appears as a physical entity. This was a big shift in Paradigms!"

In this light of inseparable unity, love may turn out to be the real fountain of youth. The abilities of love to heal, to restore, to sustain us are unrivaled. Where love is - there is the goodness in which life thrives.

Love is deeper in its mysteries than the deepest ocean. We are only at the beginning of our understanding of the hidden, unseen domains that still lie dormant in most human beings. Astounding stories from those who die and come back and share their visions of other worlds with us, often speak of the immensity and penetrating quality of love that seems to move in the "other worlds."

STRESS AND LOVING OURSELVES

Awakening our ageless nature requires a never ending ability to renew, to refresh, to restore and to stay intimately connected to our "life principle." The vibrant independence needed is often triggered by difficulties and challenges. Growing is not stress free. However, in the current climate of so many people wanting to love themselves more, there is a tendency to remove anything stressful as an "act of compassion" for themselves. This is misguided and based on a one-sided understanding of stress and its effects on our wellbeing.

The extremely popular TED talk by, researcher and author, Kelly McGonigal, presents a side of stress that has all but been forgotten by our society. "Stress," she argues, "can be your friend."

Twelve and a half million people have seen this talk, and a broader understanding of two sides of stress is emerging now. Bad stress and good stress. Eustress or the beneficial stress is the stress of challenges that unlock our latent gifts and powers. It is the trigger that excites, stimulates action or shakes up our comfortable habits. The following question is from her insightful book, *The Upside of Stress:*

> "What is the cost of avoiding stress ? Although avoiding stress can seem like a rational strategy, it almost always backfires. One of the benefits of embracing stress is that you find the strength to pursue goals and endure experiences that are difficult but meaningful."

There are other important questions. Are there things you would like to do or experience if only you were not so afraid of the stress it might cause? Would your life be enriched by pursuing any of these? What's the cost of stopping yourself from pursue them? The price we pay may be very high for thinking that avoiding and removing stress is always a good thing. For many well-meaning people this "act of self-love" may turn out to be an act of self-sabotage. Loving ourselves also means to be engaged in meaningful, self-actualizing activities. Ask yourself, "Is my compassionate love towards myself opening me to life or is it shielding me from opportunities to grow? Is the garden of my heart in need of a fence or fresh, unexpected rain and new plants to diversify the beauty of its life-giving power?"

Stress can be detrimental to our health, but I feel we may have overlooked the healthy benefits of stress. Certainly the constriction of our adventurous spirit is not in alignment with a creating a life of ongoing meaning.

The aging model is painted in graphic detail by a lifeless and uninspired materialistic culture. This belief system has us maturing steadily to middle age and then over we go to the side of the aging hill, which goes downhill steadily until we eventually die. "I'm over the hill now," people say all too often. But what are they really saying? Is it "I have peaked in my life," or "my best is behind me now?" And what of the so called twilight years? What is this implying? This label reveals what is being programmed in your mind. You are being conditioned to believe the *twilight years* are the years during which your light gradually fades and sets, like the sun setting on the horizon of your life.

What nonsense this is! I recently saw a film of a beautiful 100 year old woman exclaiming after a run with her friend, "I'm over the hill and only picking up speed." The active lives of the world's centenarians are not stress free, they do not eat special food, nor do they live removed from society. The research from the last twenty years is showing that they are living lives that are meaningful in an ongoing way. They stay committed to the loving relationships they nurture and they stay resilient by believing they belong as vital members of their culture. They are not isolated or taken care of. They are valued by those around them. They still participate, not only as an equal to everyone else but often rise up to become wisdom figures actively guiding many around them. Aging becomes meaningless. Life is full of meaning for them and that is what they stay focused on.

Stress and Love go together in our living agelessly. Here are a few more insights from Kelly McGonigal about stress from the growing number of research studies now emerging.

> *"Stress is harmful, except when it's not.*
> *Stress increases the risk of health problems, except*
> *when people regularly give back to their*
> *communities.*
> *Stress increases the risk of dying, except when people*
> *have a sense of purpose.*
> *Stress increases the risk of depression, except when*
> *people see the benefit in their struggles."*

For every harmful outcome you can think of, there's an exception that erases the expected association between stress and something bad and replaces it with an unexpected benefit.

LIGHT THERAPY

As a little girl of 8, I had my first experiences with UV light therapy. Of course I knew nothing of the newly emerging science that was taking root in German medical practices. All I knew was that I enjoyed the adventure sitting for 30 minutes at a time in front of a large machine, wearing my dark glasses and feeling the light envelop my face. The long winter months in the northern part of Germany were not only cold but cloudy and dark. Our family doctor prescribed regular sessions of UV light therapy to build Vitamin D naturally and I was promised that I would not get sick like so many of my classmates and for the most part I never did. "No virus can take a hold of you and you will have strong bones," he would say. I was delighted to spend all winter healthy enjoying time outside with my sleigh. The doctor made it fun for me and I remember even now the UV light that left me with beautiful rosy cheeks every time I left his office. Gabriel Cousens, M.D. wrote in his foreword to the book, *Light Years Ahead*:

"We are human photocells whose ultimate biological nutrient is light. Food, through the process of photosynthesis, brings sunlight energy in the form of resonating electrically active carbon-carbon bonds and electron clouds on double-bonded structures into our physical bodies. This light is then released into our systems as electrical energy. It also stimulates an equal and opposite release of the inner light."

Phototherapy or Light Therapy has a long and fascinating history of applications all over the world. It is currently associated with the holistic models of wellness that involve ways to stimulate and balance the individual's unique vital energy. Wellness is very different from the absence of pathology. It is a state that includes the individual's physical, emotional, cognitive, spiritual and social responsibility.

Light therapy is now being seen in different ways as brain models and the functioning of sight take on more integrated roles. They are now seen as affecting each other in far more complex ways as previously known. This is exemplified by the statements of Jacob Lieberman, OD.,Ph.D. who wrote "How is it that we see? What's going on? When I went to school, we had the idea that the way that vision worked was that information entering the eye went back into the computer, and the computer inverted the picture. Professors made it sound as though it was something like a camera and then, through some magic, we saw. We all understood the neurology, physiology, and so on, but we were never told how it is we see."

This is exactly the understanding I grew up with in Germany. Our eyes were simply where the light entered, was focused and captured. Nothing more was questioned. The light was triggering cells that sent signals back to the brain. Eyes were organs of the senses and the brain a completely separate organ. Not content with this as an explanation of how exactly we actually see, Dr. Lieberman goes on to state,

> *"What I discovered quite a few years ago is something about how it is that we see. The eyes are always making these micro movements. The eyes are situated right at the helm of this system. The eyes are not a separate entity from the brain - they are the brain. The brain has two frontal extensions called eyes. When light strikes the eye, it simultaneously strikes the brain. The eyes and the brain are the same."*

Much research is being conducted into the workings of our sight and the role light plays in our lives. I have discovered a group of researchers in France who have launched a company to create and distribute an advanced light therapy device that is unrivaled in its technical achievements. I use it regularly to enhance my states of mind. The screens of its light glasses are capable of very rapid full spectrum light variations that are coordinated by a micro -computer built into the frames. Through various "light shows" these glasses support the brain to generate a full spectrum of brain waves, alpha, beta, delta and theta. The light therapy programs are designed to support morning, afternoon and evening activities.

The company was named PSIO and is based in Paris; and they are building a distribution network now in the US. I use it in combination with my BEMER treatments for a full energetic rejuvenation or deep relaxation. You can learn more on my website: www.AgelesstheBook.com/PSIO.

POTS AND PANS
Tools We Cook With

"You are NOT what you eat,
you are what you digest and assimilate."
~ Tony Robbins

Any professional will tell you the quality of the tools they use plays a significant role in the results they achieve. For some, such as doctors, the tools they use every day must meet very high material standards. For instance, the metals used in the various tools in an operating room are of high quality steel, yet an even higher quality of steel is used in metal hip replacements and other metal pins which remain for years in human bodies. These metal alloys even though expensive cannot be replaced by lesser metals. There are large amounts of research now on how metals react to human tissues and cells.

How does this relate to the tools we cook with you may wonder? Well, almost all our primary cooking tools are made of metal alloys, which most of us are not well educated about. In the US, cookware is completely unregulated, so many products made with metals and coatings that are banned from use in other countries are sold here with the naive perception that they are perfectly safe because they are *in the marketplace*. But nothing could be further from the truth. Many are leaching highly toxic poisons directly into our food and millions of well meaning families who are buying quality 'organic' foods are tragically compromising their own health and the wellbeing of their families. Shoddy companies pushing shoddy goods on an uninformed population is shameful and unprofessional.

Not only are we, as a nation, poorly educated about nutrition, but even our doctors, on average, still receive less than 10 hours of nutritional education during their entire 4-6 years of medical school and internships. Only the very highest quality cookware is free from leaching damaging heavy metals and toxic chemicals into your food every time you cook. You may be inadvertently poisoning yourselves and your families. This poisoning, because it is ongoing, can have very serious consequences. Therefore, I highly recommend that you educate yourself on the materials you use to cook with and get familiar with the various health and safety issues. These are tools you use everyday and you need to be aware of the quality or lack of quality they possess. On my website I have a section where I discuss where to find accurate research on this subject and recommend the finest cookware to invest in. www.AgagelesstheBook.com/cooking

High quality metals can also dramatically affect what happens to the nutrition in our foods, before, during and after cooking. Often, the simple overheating of our foods in the cooking process can destroy and rob us of over 90% of the nutritional benefit. It takes some education to discover the art of cooking with quality metal cookware so that you maintain the optimum nutritional value and have no leaching of toxic metals and chemicals. I can assure you it is well worth the effort. Not only will you have more strength and vitality but in using only high quality metal cookware you will delight every time you use it, knowing that you are safe and have stopped the slow poisoning coming from inferior products. I feel it is tragic that companies which have their products banned because of proven health risks in other countries would go on to sell them in 'unregulated' countries such as the United States.

DISTANCE HEALING

With regard to one last aspect of energy and the new ways we are employing it, I want to share a few thoughts regarding distance healing - which also has a rich history of success. Here too, new models of reality are needed to support your efforts to make sense of these seemingly impossible healing methods. It turns out that not only is space transcended, having no significance whatsoever, but that time is also of no significance and the beneficial effects are instantaneously manifested. My friend Eileen McKusick, a pioneer in what she terms Biofield Tuning, reports that distance healing for individuals is repeatedly effective. It is also effective with entire groups of people who are in various locations around the world at the time of the sessions. She has an ongoing series of remote group healings that she conducts from her office in Vermont. Her groundbreaking book, *Tuning the Human Biofield,* traces the history of the discoveries of the biofield in plants, animals and humans, and sets forth many foundations upon which the tuning practices, primarily done with tuning forks, can be employed. You can learn more about her on my website at: www.agelessthebook.com/biofield

We are living in a universe that may be far more interconnected than it is possible to ever comprehend. Biofield energy and its role in healing is a fast developing area of research and therapeutic practice.

In the next chapter we will explore how important community is on your journey to live agelessly. I will share with you some of the mistakes which cost me years of progress. I hope you may learn some of these hard won lessons, take them to heart and have the courage to act now and claim your birthright to thrive in health, longevity and success at any age.

Chapter 4

THE AGELESS LIVING REVOLUTION

WHY THE CENTENARIANS MATTER

A change in biology and a change in economics are going to transform our world in the next few decades. The change in biology is easily understood in the extension of human lifespans and the quality with which those extensions will be enjoyed. The other is a bit more complex in that the economic landscapes of every society will be reshaped by the changing demographics of a new generation of mature, vibrant and contributing human beings who are thriving well past 100 years of age.

I call this the coming ageless revolution. The stages of any revolution are dissatisfaction, frustration, demoralization and then outright revolt. Hopefully this revolution will be replacing the conditions that led to the problem with new structures, ideas and people to lead the way to new ways of being. A proactive approach is needed if you are to program your new ageless mind in new ways of believing, thinking, feeling and valuing.

In the diagram below there are 13 characteristics. Each of these has been shown, in study after study, to be central to meaningful and healthy longevity.

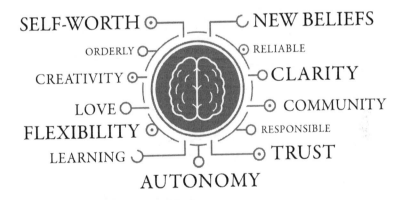

PROGRAM YOUR AGELESS MIND

SELF-WORTH — NEW BELIEFS
ORDERLY — RELIABLE
CREATIVITY — CLARITY
LOVE — COMMUNITY
FLEXIBILITY — RESPONSIBLE
LEARNING — TRUST
AUTONOMY

There is, at present massive pressure building from the disconnect between the fastest growing segment of populations, centenarians! That's right - people over 80 are the fastest growing segment of populations worldwide. And if the cutting-edge scientists, leading the biomedical revolution in life extension are successful you will be seeing humans living over 150 years sooner than you may think.

RESILIENCE AND CREATIVITY ARE ATTRIBUTES OF CENTENARIANS AROUND THE WORLD,

This growing population is faced with a dilemma. The current model of aging has them isolated firmly in nursing homes in their "twilight years" by the time they get close to 90, but many of them are seeing another possibility. Not only are they seeing another life, but they are taking active steps to reshape the "healthy image" of more mature human beings. The health craze of the 80's and 90's will pale in comparison to the stunning powers of human beings who free themselves from the tired and outdated models of human health with its mechanical limitations and shortsighted, reductionist understandings of the human body/mind.

A boomer generation is already shaking up the old ideas of aging. As of this writing, Mick Jagger is out on tour, still delivering electrifying performances at 75 that would exhaust most musicians half his age. Artists and musicians, dancers, actors and filmmakers have always thrived in old age; but what of the local baker, the accountant, the gardener who says "No!" to succumbing to a slow, isolating, downward journey? These courageous people will emerge in the millions to reshape the world as we know it today. It is my sincere hope that you will be one of them.

AGELESS TIP
CHOOSE ONE

The <u>Ageless</u> Life

The <u>Aging</u> Life

I predict that, as a society, we will no longer be stamping out labels to define mature human beings that are demoralizing, degrading and downright destructive. New ways of thinking are not just new ways of thinking "about" your body as if it is a machine. New ways of thinking, perceiving, embodying and feeling will literally become your sculpting tools. In your hands these tools will shape the ageless human beings that will serve as the role models for so many who need inspiration and guidance. You will embody the new "elder" in ways undreamt of in the past. You will know that each thought is capable of becoming cascades of chemical structures, each feeling altering their biofield, each perception creating not only their personal experience but literally sending out "commands" that the "living field" will use to shape reality for the next adventure in expansion. The assurance that the actual space in which your body is embedded is alive with limitless potential will set a new stage for the endless advance in the unlocking of your human powers. Powers of belief, perception and experiences. You, as human being struggling to stay alive, to last, can become an everlasting being through expanding past the limitations of your spatial body and individual life-span. All you need for this is imagination and empathy.

A NEW VIEW OF LONGEVITY

"The imagination is the golden pathway to everywhere."
~ Terence McKenna

In imagining a new way of thinking about living longer, we are extending the *idea* of longevity itself. The idea of longevity has been held in our scientific world-view to be primarily a physiological issue. Simply put, our bodies can and will live longer and longer. Long life is long life of the body. Any other considerations are not a part of our discussions. Why is this? What has happened to us? We have failed as a society to support the meaning of a long life as it is lived by a real human being. In extending this idea we need to broaden it and deepen it. Mark Twain said, "You can't depend on your eyes when your imagination is out of focus." Our understandings of longevity are woefully out of focus. This lack of clarity and temporary impairment in vision are having massive and deadly consequences for individuals living into their 60's, 70's, 80's, 90's and 100's in every part of our world.

Earlier in humanity's understanding of longevity there was a rich collection of philosophic and religious ideas associated with living a long life. There were myriads of myths, stories and rituals which gave longevity rich and powerful meaning. The journey through life was undertaken by a "soul," not merely a body. There was a ripening "character" moving through the stages of life who was connected to the forces and influences of Gods, Goddesses, Muses, Saints and Prophets. Uniqueness was seen as a valuable gift to be cultivated and ripened.

The long life could be a mythic life, an adventurous life, a romantic life, a courageous life, a tragic life or a tapestry of many lives woven into the life of a truly seasoned "elder." To live long and live well were possible in the richly developed character of a unique individual who was consciously aware of living in an intelligent Cosmos. This Cosmos was populated with forces, powers and beings that both uplifted and inspired, as well as forces, powers and beings which could test, challenge or defeat. It was not a world of empty space, big bangs, black holes and space/time continuums. Many now believe that our current obsession with physics has taken us completely in the wrong direction in our search for knowledge and led to a dead end. It is your choice to create the world you live in or to accept the view of "authorities" who will be happy to create it for you.

Your imagination is not even remotely what our spiritually bankrupt culture would have you believe. It is not hindered by the demeaning assertions that physical reality is all that matters and that "getting real" is an ideal. These dead fruits of a material age have merely clouded over the power and value of imagination and its place in your life. You have been stripped of the richest tool to enliven, broaden and deepen your life. The state of spiritual poverty that afflicts so many who are entering their extra decades of life is staggering in its scale, complex and confusing in its causes and baffling in its solutions. We arrived at this state as a culture. A culture that has defined aging in ways that are far too narrow, too shallow and too simplistic. This is what needs attention and needs to change. But how? Where shall we look? C. S. Lewis wrote, "Reason is the natural order of truth; but imagination is the organ of meaning." If we are to change the meaning of longevity we need imagination.

I propose you return imagination to play a powerful and central role in your life again. Imagination and empathy work together. Tolerating our current conditions and failing to be empathetic toward the lonely, the demented, the isolated and meaningless lives being lived out across the world, is ultimately a failure of imagination. Our culture will progress very differently with a different attitude toward imagination. "The true sign of intelligence is not knowledge but imagination," said Albert Einstein. We also need, desperately need, a resurrection of philosophic thinking that transforms and frees "aging" from its narrow thought prison. Longevity will only be an idea that is vital, meaningful and adventurous when our philosophy and our worldview, our cosmology, is vital, meaningful and adventurous. That will require a return to a philosophically and imaginatively rich culture. James Hillman, the American psychologist and author wrote in *The Force of Character*, "If you would find decrepitude and rectify it, then look to the culture and begin with the rigor mortis of its skeptical and analytical philosophies and the loneliness and dementia of its imagination."

Here is an example of how this resurrection of the power of imagination can breathe life in our relationships.

"If the character of a person is a complexity of images, then to know you I must imagine you, absorb your images. To stay connected with you, I must stay imaginatively interested, not in the process of our relationship or in my feelings for you, but in my imaginings of you. The connection through imagination yields an extraordinary closeness. Where imagination focuses intently on the character of the other — as it does between opposing generals, guard and hostage, analyst and patient — love follows.

The human connection may benefit from exhortations to love one another, but for a relationship to stay alive, love alone is not enough. Without imagination, love stales into sentiment, duty, boredom. Relationships fail not because we have stopped loving but because we have stopped imagining." ~ James Hillman

AGELESS

ELDERS AND CHARACTER

Is there a role to be played in human society that deepens and enriches the life of all? What if the old are seen as living representations of a valuable, ancient archetype: oldness? Oldness gives added value and luster to things we treasure, places we revere, and people's character. Many societies held just such roles in high esteem. The treasured histories of a family, tribe or nation were often embodied in human beings whose lives and stories brought these treasures to life. They held these in ways that the young could not because they were rich in insights, imagination, perspective. Their lives were woven into the actual tapestry of the tradition or history.

Even in our individual modern lives we play this role. "Every man is his own ancestor, and every man is his own heir. He devises his own future, and he inherits his own past," said Frederick Henry Hedge. However, the scope and depth of playing the role of elder, when rooted in a unique culture, tribe or tradition, takes on a power that is transcendent. It is not confined to the physical life of the individual. The role "embodies" the history and meaning for the rest of the group to see and witness its living force in their midst. The individual's life as an elder is extended backwards in time.

"Growing into the roots of traditions
lengthens life backwards."
~James Hillman

I am aware of the failure to "motivate" mature people to engage in activities designed to keep them younger looking, fitter and more energetic. Motivating women to take care of themselves and their skin is also only partially effective. This tendency to assume that motivation is needed is misdirected and based on a lack of understanding of human character.

> *"He is the true enchanter, whose spell operates, not upon the senses, but upon the imagination and the heart."* ~ Washington Irving, America's first international best-selling author.

Your own inner voice is more than enough to guide you to action when it is aligned with your highest values. Clarifying and prioritizing your highest values and then committing to and aligning with these values leads you to a feeling of fulfillment, excitement and satisfaction. The prodding and motivation, so common in our efforts at self-improvement are no longer needed. You are then self-actualizing and autonomous. "The power of imagination makes us infinite," said John Muir. Popular assumptions that "aging" is caused by cellular problems, molecular failure and chemical imbalances are propagated by many in the field of gerontology. These proclaimed and highly visible "causes" are only half the story and most likely the least important half. Human beings developing lives that have character, power and purpose has been swept away in our rush to "fix" human bodies to last longer. The problem is a simple one. Your molecular scientist is interested in your DNA, your molecular health and cellular abilities to replicate successfully. Our society has simply permitted the "cellular expert" to dominate the conversation and no other voices are heard. That is what needs to change and change quickly.

We are so obsessed with doing that we have no time and no imagination left for being. As a result, men are valued not for what they are but for what they do or what they have - for their usefulness.
~Thomas Merton

Lasting longer, with a public disregard for the deepening of character, strengthening of imagination, and increasing the sense of life's meaning is not addressing the needs of our souls. Simply lasting longer is a goal that is missing the point of your human life. By aiming in a direction that ignores the deeper meanings of living longer lives altogether we will continue to have a culture that continues to support dysfunctional aging beliefs. The redirecting of our attention to enriching our vision of life's purpose in the later years can unlock the hidden meanings in our body's changes in radically different ways.

A great wind is blowing, and that gives you either imagination or a headache.
~ Catherine the Great

The physiological view of your body moving through time is not capable of addressing the unfolding needs and desires of your soul's evolution and the deepening of your imagination to provide a path to ageless living. This is living that is redefining longevity as an opportunity to extend our lives in meaning, in depth, in significance, in strength of character, and in the many attributes of a soul.

Keep in mind that "ancestors" and the old ones in past societies were often young people by our measure. The average lifespan for tens of thousands of years was eighteen. So people in their thirties were most likely the elders and carriers of the traditions and myths. They were the storytellers and healers. Numerical age is not what defines an elder. What defines them are character and depth of soul, imagination and philosophy, insight and empathy.

WHAT IS ON THE HORIZON

What kind of revolution are you going to experience when millions of human beings begin to live lives that contain the wisdom of what today would be two lifetimes, then three lifetimes? Creating a new vision of a future for this new group is of the utmost importance: a future that is capable of supporting the dreams and hopes of people still healthy and vital at 65, at 85 and beyond. What kinds of roles will they play when new ways of thinking about maturing well are developed and adopted? What roles will you play? Fun is one motivation to be sure. Having worked for a lifetime many feel the need to enjoy life more. But creating meaning and value is also very significant and the idea of retirement as a time to kick back and relax is being replaced with the idea of this stage of life as a time of opportunity. The dawning revolution of ageless living is well underway. The use of the arts in conjunction with the far reaching powers of the internet are already bringing completely new forms of social change in this area.

ONE BILLION RISING

The recent dancing that marked the international social movement to end violence toward women, One Billion Rising, set the world ablaze with emotion and empowerment. Men and women alike were transfixed by the images flooding in from over 150 countries of women dancing passionately to raise this urgently needed call in all parts of the world. Artistically engaging hundreds of thousands of women to share a dance of protest, on the very same day, in every corner of earth, had never happened before, and this was just the beginning. Mature women danced alongside younger women and girls, victims of the violence danced with those seeking forgiveness and redemption, children danced too and the world saw something it had not ever seen before. A world -wide problem with its overwhelming scale was being met and healed by a world-wide response, a big response, a response big enough to actually change the situation. A new quality of hope was felt. This, I believe, is what sent shivers of spirit down the spines of so many. We were seeing an emerging power of the human race. A power we "shared." Taught to think we are all separate individuals and inherently separated, this taught us a different lesson. We share this power. We share this in unity and love.

What kind of revolution is forming where we share in the reshaping of human life itself? The 100 year old woman in the US who says, "I'm over the hill and still picking up speed," is heard by her friend in person but; when her friend uploads a video of her to YouTube things change. She is now heard by thousands of other women and men and they reframe their lives and they start "picking up speed." What happens when a 100 year old breaks the 4 minute mile? The old paradigms of aging may drop away much faster than anyone can foresee.

Add to all this ever more instantaneous communications, ever improved natural foods, ever bigger dreams, perfected biomedical life extenders and the world will be in for a shock of unimaginable proportions. This is all on the horizon and is, I believe, a reason to celebrate the coming ageless living revolution. What is normal today will seem hideously barbaric to future generations. For us to lock away our elders, to drug them, to shame them, to condemn them to irrelevant and meaningless lives, lived in front of impersonal TV's will be unthinkable in the near future.

AGELESS

WHAT IS GOING ON TODAY

Ten percent of the residents in assisted living
facilities are 65 or younger, revealing the shocking truth
about our collective health. Forty percent of all residents in
nursing homes never have visitors, illustrating the callousness
of our collective consciousness. We have numbed ourselves
into the false belief that "they" are cared for by
"professional" caregivers. Profound isolation and alienation
is a way of life for millions of people in our so-called
advanced civilizations. Just how advanced are we after all?
When Gandhi was asked what he thought of western
civilization, he replied, "I think it would be a good idea."

Endless statistics are being gathered about our
aging populations that tell us nothing about the changes
ahead. They focus on diseases, age limits, physiological
profiles, locations, demographics, drug use and not on what
is stirring in the hearts of millions of mature citizens who are
about to change the world. This stirring in the heart and the
changes that will swiftly transform our society is a revolution
of huge proportions that will be tracked in the future,
measured and studied by the same folks who are missing it
today.

I am so determined to change this world, one
hurting soul at a time. We are not separate from the
suffering, we are not separate from the lonely, we are not safe
and removed in our homes with our families and loved ones
around us. It is we who are living in these nursing "homes." It
is we who are drugged. It is we who are staring at the TV's

for endless hours as the world moves on without us. We are suffering this degradation. It is we who are deadened and living the lives of lost and forgotten souls cared for by strangers. I am not OK with any of these conditions, and see them as not serving the well-being of life on earth. Can we really welcome new life into this world of callousness and fear? Are the newborn feeling the hearty welcome to life that would be extended by a healthy society? I see the hesitation in new mothers and fathers as they question the quality of life their children may have. I sense the ambivalence around the future we are creating for our children. The problems with the economy and so-called lack of opportunities are overshadowed by the deeper moral problems of relegating millions of people to lives of utter meaninglessness, perpetuating the lie of aging as a given. Living a long life is far from the downward slope you have been conditioned to believe. It possibly never was true. A strange mixture of mechanistic medical practices, short-sighted business interests and misguided scientists has led to our current model of aging.

The beliefs about aging are so powerful that they still keeps millions of people ensnared in a hypnotic trance. Light hypnotic suggestions or deep, powerful trances still render you helpless to fully awaken to the miracle of your life. The tragedy is that these prisons of belief have been entered freely. The doors have no locks. There are no guards and yet the inmates are convinced they belong there and seek no escape. Philosopher Michel Foucault warned us that societal controls are so deeply embedded in our consciousness that we function as if we were in a fish tank, unable to see the glass that contains us. Nevertheless, many of you waking up from this collective nightmare. I hope my voice will help inspire you to never again slip into the trance-like slumber of giving up on life and letting yourselves be tricked into surrendering your vitality, purpose and usefulness. Is it attractive to be a zombie in someone else's movie? Go out on the streets and tell me if you do not see many people asleep to the greatness within them, numb to the deep springs of infinite compassion that is their birthright and dead to the love that is their destiny to radiate from their hearts. Yet there they are walking upright - on their way - zombies in a movie they are acting in for someone else. I guarantee you that if they were awake to the fact that it is actually their own movie they are "starring in," they would not choose to play a supporting role, let alone play the part of a zombie.

I am being overly dramatic here because I feel there actually is a problem. And this is a problem that is inside you and me. The covering over of your greatness, your mystery, your purpose, your stunning complexity have blinded you to something fundamental about human beings. Our transcendent powers of thought, elevated emotions and unique gifts have been trapped for centuries in cultural ideologies that no longer serve us. I invite you to question these for yourselves. I have been surprised at how many assumptions I left unchallenged, way past the time these beliefs were serving my progress. I have been helped by skilled coaches like Dr. Jean Houston, Tony Robbins and most recently Matt Kahn, who called this process "Shaking up the snow globe of your world." Let's shake it up together and together find the courage and power to dance our way to a wealthy new world of ageless living.

> "The most powerful weapon on earth
> is the human soul on fire."
> ~Ferdinand Foch

Resilience is a core attribute of your Ageless Life.

Pablo Picasso said, "I'm always doing that which I cannot do, in order that I may learn how to do it."

A NEW WORLD OF SUBCULTURES

Plotinus wrote, in the third century, more like a modern physics professor than a scholar at the beginning of the last millennium. Perhaps his insight radiates across time in a deeper way than we can see at present with our "modern eyes."

"See all things, not in process of becoming, but in being, and see themselves in each other. Each being contains in itself the whole intelligible world. Therefore All is everywhere. Each is their All, and All is each. Man as he now is has ceased to be the All. But when he ceases to be an individual, he raises himself again and penetrates the whole world."

The support we need to make these changes is both internal support and the support of a circle of friends; these are what Dr. Mario Martinez calls subcultures of wellness. He states:

"To create sustainable change, you need cultural support. ...Subcultures of wellness are those that explore the ways individual excellence can contribute to collective abundance. Your focus shifts away from remaining within the pale that keeps you

trapped in collective known misery, and shifts toward freedom from the pale..."

It is a blessing to stand and explore in a circle of friends who are committed to change and determined to shape a better future for all in that circle. With a quality of empathetic joy uplifting your efforts and accomplishments, this subculture forms a social foundation that supports your actions that challenge the old paradigms of "aging." In the next chapter I will share with you some of my experiences with these growing subcultures. They are also a setting in which the exalted emotions are shared. These emotions play a huge role in supporting the coming ageless revolution.

"I define the exalted emotions as effects with a foundation in love" Dr. Martinez writes. "They include compassion, empathy, admiration, generosity, gratitude, magnanimity, and any other emotion that expresses our human dignity."

THE FORCES AGAINST THE REVOLUTION

Where has our culture's "scientific knowledge" of aging come from? For the most part all the physical and psychological knowledge has come from the experimental sciences. Endless medical studies, university experiments, big-data analysis run on big company computers, etc. However there is a problem here.

In the words of Spanish philosopher Ortega y Gasset,

> *"It is necessary to insist upon this extraordinary but undeniable fact: experimental sciences have progressed thanks in great part to the work of men astoundingly mediocre, and even less than mediocre. That is to say, modern science, the root and symbol of our actual civilization, finds a place for the intellectually commonplace man that allows him to work therein with success."*

I am not saying we disregard all this research as being done by "less than mediocre" minds. What I am suggesting is that we realize that the experimental sciences are very limited in giving us any insights into what is possible in the areas of human potential. Many so called "cutting edge" experiments are designed to "prove" what has been obvious to greater minds for centuries. Ellen Langer, a Harvard professor, has conducted some of the more fascinating studies that look at reversing age through mindfulness and environments designed to "turn back our cultural clock."

She writes "The more we realize that most of our views about ourselves, of others, and of presumed limits regarding our talents, our health, and our happiness were mindlessly accepted by us at an earlier time in our lives, the more we open up to the realization that these too can change. And all we need to do is begin the process 'to be mindful.'"

EMBRACING A NEW FUTURE

Creating a future for ourselves that includes staying engaged and happy for the long lives we are living will be one of the most vital roles we play. This is the very beginning of an era of challenges that will mold how the generations after us will think and feel about human life. Considering that for the last one hundred thousand years of human history most people had lifespans that lasted only 18 years. Radical changes will rock the world simply because of this new reality. You stand at the very beginning of a new human era. What you feel about this future being thrust on you is going to make all the difference. If you fear it, you may recoil from creative action and allow the deficient medical system and other social institutions to simply be patching up a sinking ship until the problems are so enormous that millions and millions of people will be impoverished in body, mind and spirit. Or you can learn to embrace the future. Yes, you stand on unknown ground and in previously unthinkable situations, and yet here you are.

At the conclusion of Rollo May's book, *Love and Will* he lays out a vision of what it means to embrace the future:

> *"We stand on the peak of the consciousness of previous ages, and their wisdom is available to us. History- that selective treasure house of the past which each age bequeaths to those that follow - has formed us in the present so that we may embrace the future. What does it matter if our insights, the new forms which play around the fringes of our minds, always lead us into virginal land where, like it or not, we stand on strange and bewildering ground? The only way out is ahead, and the choice is whether we shall cringe from it or affirm it. For in every act of love and will - and in the long run they are both present in each genuine act - we mold ourselves and our world simultaneously. This is what it means to embrace the future."*

Embracing your future lies first in understanding that the only way out of this unfamiliar world lies ahead of you. You are formed in the present to embrace the future and as you embrace it you are changing yourself and your world at the same time. I invite you to be bold and creative in your embrace of the changes ahead. It is for you to design and implement the new stories, rituals, careers and explorations that your longer life will hold.

Initiate from your generous nature!

Don't be afraid to express the generous invitations your heart may be inspired to offer. Listen closely to those tender wishes and speak them out loud. Make your offers and invitations and then suspend all judgement. Don't anticipate the responses. Trust and listen. You may be astonished at what comes back to you.

DESIGN YOUR OWN NEW AGELESS LIVING RITUALS, PARTIES. LUNCHEONS AND DINNERS

"Sometimes you have to move on without certain people. If they're meant to be in your life, they'll catch up."
~Mandy Hale

Here is a personal ageless living ritual you may want to bring into your life. It is meditation for healing the relationship you have with your body, your "Magical Temple."

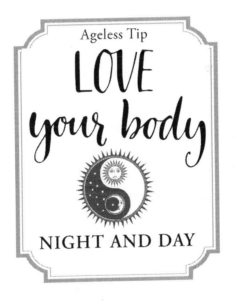

A LOVING MEDITATION WITH YOUR BODY

Forgive me that I ignored you so much of our life together.
That will change.
Forgive my ignorance toward your needs.
That will change.
Forgive me that I often took you for granted.
That will change.
I apologize for the water I deprived you of.
That will change.
I apologize that I barely exercise you to stay strong and flexible.
That will change.

THANK YOU FOR YOUR DEVOTION TO KEEP ME
HEALTHY AND FUNCTIONAL, DESPITE THE
NEGLECT I HAVE SHOWN TOWARDS YOU.

PLEASE ACCEPT MY HEARTFELT APOLOGIES.

I was numb and blind - I wasn't aware - I didn't feel -
I was just like one in billions - running through time and space -
missing the importance and magic between you and I.

MY PROMISE TO YOU,
MY MIRACULOUS TEMPLE IS THIS:

I promise you
I will pay closer attention and learn your language,
so you can hear what you need.

AGELESS

I promise you
I will learn to nourish you with the best,
healthiest food for our peak condition.

I promise you
to always have quality water within reach.

I promise you
I will start our day with exercise.

I promise you
I will honor the time you need and surrender to sleep. So that
you can work through the night to repair and balance all the
wear and tear from the day. When you enable me to open my
eyes, I will be refreshed, protected, strong, happy and vital to
conquer our new day together.

THANK YOU

I am in awe - I am in deep gratitude - I am feeling so blessed to
have the honor to live within you, my "Magical Temple."

I LOVE YOU

I encourage you to compose your own rituals, "outside of
normal time" and the routines of daily life. Private rituals and
social rituals will nourish your resilience and provide the soul
food necessary for real and lasting transformation. Invite others

to join you in the ageless living revolution. Celebrate together, learn together and be in sacred space together.

In the next chapter I will share with you the powerful ways in which sub-cultures of learning are providing the vision of a future in which people are molding themselves and their world simultaneously.

Here we will see the fourth key to a miraculous life at any age come into focus. Remember that you are never alone on your soul's journey through life. The isolation and loneliness that crush so many souls today will, I pray, soon be lifted and replaced by a compassion so strong, so universal that not one soul will be left to suffer this condition. You are never alone. Ask for help, offer support, participate in life with others and feel your spirit soar and grow in ways completely and delightfully unexpected.

These ageless living communities have been created by a new kind of leader. These leaders are responding to the new realities of second or third careers, reinvented lives, inquiring souls who are seeking spiritual meaning and communion with others. The needs are new, the land is virginal that you stand on. We have not been here before and the guidance is not yet created to help steer us successfully in any tried and true way. So I invite you to affirm yourself, trust yourself and create, invent and love your way into your embrace of the future.

Chapter 5

AGELESS LIVING COMMUNITIES

The first time I was with Dr. Jean Houston in the rolling hills of Petaluma California, she defined the word entelechy as "the deep purpose that guides your becoming." I had never heard the word before but it rang from her with an unusual power, as if the word itself held magic. It entered my heart with a mysterious force. Entelechy was for me a revelation. It seemed to sum up that primal combination of forces within each of us that both knows and guides at the same time.

In one of her exercises Jean said, "The Essential Self knows the possible paths our life may take and wants to help us choose the best ones. It knows how to turn imagination into reality and make the life we live fulfilling and creative. Above all, it knows why we are here and what we yet can do; where we can go and why we need to go there."

In our work together it became increasingly clear as the days unfolded that the small group of us journeying with her in our transformational cocoon, removed temporarily from our daily distractions and pressures, were engaging our "entelechy." We were experiencing a mysterious knowing and guidance amplified that expanded as the unity of our group matured. We were becoming a unified "field", and she was guiding not just us individually now, but directing the 'we' that had emerged. Swept up in this loving atmosphere I felt my heart restored, my body energized, my mind expanded and my spirit reconnected to the shared Source of Life. This experience changed forever my perspectives and understanding of why working in groups can be so powerful. I also learned to recognize the unique gift that Dr. Houston has. She is so attractive and radiates so much hope and inspiration as she shares her visions of our connection to life in it's mysterious efforts to love and support us. We are never alone. Once again this key insight unlocked in me an ageless potency that was in me and beyond me. One thing was for sure. I am not alone.

Deirdre Lovecky, in her book, Warts and Rainbows: Issues in the Psychotherapy of the Gifted states, "Derived from the Greek word for having a goal, entelechy is a particular type of motivation, need for self-determination, and an inner strength and vital force directing life and growth to become all one is capable of being. Gifted people with entelechy are often attractive to others who feel drawn to their openness and to their dreams and visions. Being near someone with this trait gives others hope and determination to achieve their own self-actualization."

In another setting, about one year later, I heard Jean say, "It would be wonderful if people could grow together in groups; teaching and learning communities where they empower, evoke and explore the enormous capacities of the human condition."

This is my vision for Ageless Living communities. They empower everyone involved, evoke the hidden resources and latent talents in each other and explore the untapped capacities inherent in each other. Doing this in communities around the world, in groups large and small, is what is needed today if you are going to shake off the cultural aging conditioning, with its pseudo comforts. You must challenge yourself to experience the discomfort of stepping out of the narrow confines of your culturally determined lifestyle. You are not alone in this. Trust yourself to find others to grow with.

I encourage you to dream and create your own unique ageless lifestyle. Listen to your own guidance and shape your communities in ways that may never have been seen on earth before. Your communities are rich in the unique wisdom, courage and information that characterize your time. These are urgently needed. You are a gifted human being who can thrive in an atmosphere of mutual support, loving company and educational enrichment.

These are some of my thoughts on the value of Ageless Living communities. Here are some thoughts on their purpose, in relation to your self-actualization?

SELF-ACTUALIZING COMMUNITIES

Ageless living must include some, if not all, of the elements of self-actualization. Self-actualization, as a concept, was first brought into use by Kurt Goldstein. He was a German neurologist and psychiatrist. His holistic approach to the human organism produced over time the principle of self-actualization, defined as the driving force that maximizes and determines the path of an individual. This later influenced the thinking of Abraham Maslow when crafting his more widely known hierarchy of human needs. Situated at the top of Maslow's "needs pyramid," self-actualization is the central need of a human being after all the other needs are met.

Recently however, in a discussion with Vishen Lakhiani, the founder of MindValley, the International Online Training Company, he said, "You know it is interesting that at the end of Maslow's life he realized there was one more. One after self-actualization." He paused and with his charismatic charm and youthful enthusiasm clearly went on to state "self-transcendence." Vishen has taken MindValley in a critically needed direction. Its purpose is to bring the wisdom of the world's best coaches and trainers in the area of human potential to people online, and recently offline in actual conferences around the world.

He also shared a vision of lifelong learning environments in which people in the future would not be isolated for four years with people their own age in one location to prepare for the "real world." Rather they would educate themselves in month long educational "colleges" that would convene in a different city every year. He envisioned the first to have Barcelona as the backdrop city and would engage teachers, coaches, artists and scientists to share their expertise in a month long intensive. Participants would do this once a year, every year of their life. This essentially would fulfill the drive for self actualization in an ongoing way. People of all ages would be engaged on this journey, and the inefficient and unproductive habit of isolating people by age would be retired for good.

"So dare to live your precious days on earth to their fullest, true to yourself, with open heart and thoughtful mind, and with the courage to change what doesn't work and accept the consequences. You may find that you can fly farther than you ever imagined."

~ Vishen Lakhiani, *The Code of the Extraordinary Mind*

I find the new research in self-actualization and its role in bringing rich meaning into our lives fascinating. Tony Robbins said: "What we can or cannot do, what we consider possible or impossible, is rarely a function of our true capability. It is more likely a function of our beliefs about who we are."

Your beliefs shape you profoundly. Beliefs that contribute to your well being and form a healthy foundation upon which to build your life have recently been an object of research around the world.

A WELLNESS MODEL

One such researcher is Professor Carol Ryff. Professor Ryff has been studying 'Well-Being' long before it was cool. For well over twenty years, she has been working to develop on new models of wellness at the University of Wisconsin-Madison. She created one of the first systematic models of Psychological Well-Being, and her model remains one of the most scientifically verified and empirically rigorous to date. Carol was motivated by the insight that well-being was a philosophical question about the meaning of a good life.

She set forth a six-part multidimensional model that encompasses a breadth of wellness that includes:

1. Positive evaluations of oneself and one's past life (Self-Acceptance),
2. A sense of continued growth and development as a person (Personal Growth)
3. The belief that one's life is purposeful and meaningful (Purpose in Life)
4. The possession of quality relations with others (Positive Relations With Others)
5. The capacity to manage effectively one's life and surrounding world (Environmental Mastery)
6. A sense of self-determination (Autonomy)

I find these six attributes or characteristics to be useful in guiding and assessing the unfoldment of an ageless living community. Wellness is complex and fluid, ever changing and, inasmuch as it includes a component of growth, is never ever able to pinned down into the "now we have it" box. Rather, you must reset your design ideas in forming communities to make sure that they stay fluid and responsive to the ever changing needs of those involved. 'That's the way we have always done things around here," I trust will soon be a statement found only in history books and comedies.

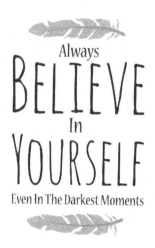

Always
BELIEVE
In
YOURSELF
Even In The Darkest Moments

And remember you are never alone.

JESSICA HADARI AND THE FEM TALKS COMMUNITY

So exactly what are self-actualizing, ageless living communities? One such community here in the San Francisco Bay Area is a good example of what is possible. My first exposure to this community, after my years of social isolation in my marriage, came as a welcome return to the rich quality of social life I had known earlier in life and knew could exist for me again. Not only did I see women and men dynamically coaching and sharing their growth and challenges in refreshing and unguarded ways, but I saw their magnetic love, vulnerability and honesty shape communities of hundreds of people around them. Soon I was able to look a bit deeper at the woman who was the organizer and nurturer at the center of this large group. A few hundred talented and professional women fall silent as Jessica Hadari takes the stage. Her words of welcome and praise set a powerful model for the assembled women to emulate. She is no simple well-wisher, nor is she naive in her task to create an ongoing community characterized by lasting friendships and associations. She is the founder of Fem Talks, bringing tireless skills and a joyful presence to shape and nurture her group.

"We believe these crucial times call for women to support, applaud, and endorse one another as we all rise up to reclaim our roles as the healers, teachers, and matriarchs of our communities and society," she writes in giving voice to her group's intentions. "We are a vibrant sisterhood of progressive women facilitators, speakers, educators, mothers, artists, life lovers and healers. It is through our diversity that we learn and grow together."

Jessica has her finger on the pulse of the change I am seeing emerge from the broken lives of thousands of women who have been isolated and frustrated. They are finding great strength and courage in committing to grow inside these loving communities and trust the guidance and direction that leaders, like Jessica Hadari, offer. She also responds to the aspirations of talented women who are stepping up to create new businesses or expand ones they already have. These leaders also function as a curator of talent, inviting guest speakers to share their knowledge and expand their influence. On the many occasions I have been with Jessica, I have always come away with new friends, renewed vision and a sense of deepened personal meaning. This kind of meaning only blooms in these living gardens of human inspiration. Some come to learn and take away something, and yet, most leave feeling as if their gifts and talents have been seen and that they have given more than they received. Jessica's value is not derived from uplifting us, even though that happens. Her real value is formed in the hearts of all those who feel seen and loved; who stand a bit taller because of her seeing of them without envy and judgment.

> THE VALUE OF A LEADER IS FOUND IN THE HEARTS OF THOSE SEEN, LOVED AND LIFTED UP BY THEM.

I am happy to say she has become a dear friend and comes to my studio regularly to share in my skills to support her. Had I not taken the risks to attend her meetings, had I stayed safe and protected from possible rejection or criticism, I would never have known just how rich the love and support can be between women who sincerely and skillfully open their hearts and talents to each other - for the benefit of all.

MIRANDA MACPHERSON AND THE AWAKENING LOVE: EMBODYING WISDOM SANGHA

Another group I am fortunate to participate in has a very different nature. This group traces its lineage back thousands of years to ancient India, and the patterns of spiritual growth that were cultivated in close knit spiritual communities. They formed sanghas in which a group journeyed together in a community. The Buddhist term sangha means sacred community. It is thought that, for full awakening, a person needs to take refuge in the Buddha (our true nature itself), the Dharma (teachings and practices that help us understand and access our true nature) and the Sangha (sacred community of like minded others with whom we can practice, learn and grow together with). This rich three-fold path that deepens our true natures, our understanding of spiritual teachings and grounds us in a community is an effective and supportive environment.

Miranda Macpherson leads such a Sangha in Marin County and in Sebastopol, California. Her lectures, sittings and inquiries support the gentle unwinding of our egoic strategies and identifications. She progressively guides her group into ever deeper expanses of self-realization and participation in Grace. Even though she is a public speaker and offers online trainings, this unique form of community benefits greatly by the "living transmission" of a skilled spiritual teacher.

Hedda Adler

Research shows that being

ORDERLY
&
RELIABLE

helps you
LIVE LONGER!

SAHAR NAFAL
AND THE BRIGHT SIDE OF LIFE COMMUNITY

There is one more community I want to share with you that has been effective in supporting thousands of women and men. It began with just six women in a living room. The intention was set and after less than a year this community grew to see monthly gatherings in the hundreds, attracting renown, motivational speakers and offering a haven of loving support year after year. It was named The Bright Side of Life by the founder of the group, Sahar Nafal. I feel honored to call her a close friend who has mentored and supported my own journey. She is always available to any of us, guiding and supporting her community. The personal development and discovery of the talents and gifts of her tribe is Sahar's passion. Her seasoned skills and huge, loving, and generous heart provide many women with the guidance and training they need in business practices to help women build community-based live events.

She also provides, month after month, the opportunities to network with hundreds of other professional women. The Bright Side of Life community events continue to open up avenues of growth to many women who feel called to initiate new chapters in their lives. Sahar helps women feel supported, educated and entertained. These big life transformations can actually be fun when done in the supportive company of kindred spirits.

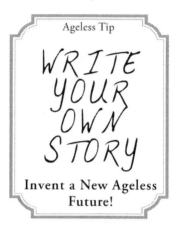

Ageless Tip

WRITE YOUR OWN STORY

Invent a New Ageless Future!

ANN RANDOLPH
Speak Your Story

Another powerful tool to transform your life is learning to refine and tell your life story. Telling your story, your life story, is the best way to build trust in your personal life and in business. I interviewed Ann Randolph over dinner recently. Ann has taught thousands of people to craft and share their life story in workshops and from the stage. Her sold-out events and performances bring to life the power of this art. Two things emerged from our discussion. The first was that your body cannot lie. Grounding and relaxing into the truth of your body to convey your story is the core of an effective transmission. The second thing she emphasized was to keep the energy of each phase of your story fresh, as if you are experiencing it for the first time. If you convey, energetically, the end of the story before it unfolds for the viewer the power of discovery is lost. Your life story, when clear and conveyed well, is one of your most powerful keys to activate your agelessness.

Ann also took a keen interest in the idea of reshaping the "aging story." A new story of ageless living could transform your compliance with the cultural messages into a new freedom that supports endless creativity and abundance. This freedom could result in building a rich understanding of ageless living wealth. Wealth of character, health, creativity, as well as financial abundance would illuminate the new and richer idea of your longevity.

GROWING WITH THE SUPPORT OF A GROUP

The Bright Side of Life community opened my eyes to the new wave of social networks that are so needed at this time. Providing the stage upon which a community can function creates more than opportunities for friendships and business relations. It forges the "entelechy" that uplifts and inspires all of us who are open to its magic to enhance the meaning of our lives. Dr. Jean Houston's encouragement to grow together in groups and create teaching and learning communities where they empower, evoke, explore the enormous capacities of the human condition is a call for action, a call for commitment and a call for transforming how we grow. Growing with the support of a group and having the opportunities to support others in a group is a powerful way to step up the progress you are making to live agelessly and say "yes" to life.

There are challenges for you that lie deep in your mind, in your bones and tissues. You have all been brought up in cultures which have planted deeply in you the messages to conform if you are to be accepted and supported inside the culture. Competition and suspicion, fears and doubts, endless variations of acceptable actions have been culturally embedded in your conscious and unconscious mind. It takes time to find, assess and cleanse yourself of the beliefs, labels and thoughts that do not serve your life. It also takes courage to free your understanding of who you are from these conditionings.

> *"People who are Happy for No Reason don't always need to figure everything out or be in control; they live in the flow of life, trusting the underlying benevolence and wisdom of that larger wholeness."*
> ~ Marci Shimoff

Stepping onto this path is much more fun and rewarding when you commit to participating in a group, or forming a group of your own. These groups require protecting and nourishing. Imagine a group that rejoices in your accomplishments; envy is replaced with empathetic joy. Empathetic joy teaches you to relish the achievements of others as your own, allowing you also to celebrate your own good fortune without any fear of banishment from the tribe or social group.

Ageless Tip

Step 1
TRUST
Step 2
ACT

TRUSTING=THRIVING!

It can begin with simple dinner parties and grow as the needs arise. Don't think you have to start big to succeed. Start where you are with your current circle of friends and just commit and invite others to commit with you. You may be, as I was, very pleasantly surprised and find your life "taking off" in directions that, at present, may be quite literally "unthinkable" for you. Trust in yourself an act.

Chapter 6

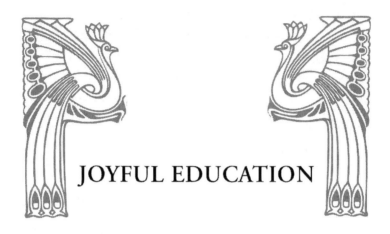

JOYFUL EDUCATION

"We live almost completely immersed in a socially constructed reality that so fully absorbs our energy and attention that virtually none remains to experience the wonder of our existence."

~Duane Elgin

Remember, you need never become a victim of "aging." Becoming a victim of aging one loses hope and joy, passion and curiosity. "What's the use? I'm too old." "I'm over the hill and not attractive anymore. Who's going to want me or love me?" These are victim thoughts. You think something is happening to you beyond your control and it's not your fault. Someone else is to blame for your state. Aging is what many women blame for what is actually their own surrender of their powerful sovereignty to decide for themselves what is happening to them.

It is crucial to realize that you need never become a victim of aging. You can remember this and reclaim your power to decide I can be victorious here. I can turn around my situation, my conditioning, my health and stand in my beauty and power. The key to not falling into the victim trap is joyful learning. Educate yourself. Assume you are an awakening genius who for a moment forgot who you were and now is speedily on the paths of mastery in any field you choose.

Your feeling of wonderment is the foundation of learning. It is the fuel for the engine of your growth and development. Without wonderment you may fall into the trap of educating yourself by taking in information and learning skills that are out of alignment with your core sense of wonder. Your dilemma, as Duane Elgin states above, may be that the "reality" you have chosen to live inside of, your socially constructed reality, is absorbing virtually all your energy. No energy remains to feel directly your wonderment of your own existence. Your efforts to educate yourself inside a reality that lacks the foundation of wonderment can lead to confusion, frustration and ultimately to apathy.

"Once you lose that sense of wonder at being alive, you're pretty much on the way out..."

-David Bowie

LEARNING AND PLAY

Education and Ecstasy, a book by George Leonard, was one of the first books to re-establish the relationship between learning and joy. Written in the 1960's, it presented a vision of learning that was in stark contrast to the industrial classrooms and rigid ideas about education at the time. It presented a vision that returned your joy to the center of your learning experience.

Experiencing the wonder of your existence is not a one time event. You cannot say, "That's it - I have truly experienced the wonder of my existence." There is an obvious problem with that thinking. The nature of your existence is ongoing, dynamic and ever changing and evolving. As such, your experiences of wonder related to your own existence needs to be ongoing and dynamic. It requires you welcoming wonder every day with renewed personal energy.

Alan Watts, the British philosopher, once stated: *"...We confuse the world as talked about, described, and measured with the world which actually is. We are sick with a fascination for the useful tools of names and numbers, of symbols, signs, conceptions and ideas."*

You have many superlatives in English that are related to wonderment. These give you the false illusion that wonderment is alive and well. How many times have you heard the words amazing, stunning, astounding, spectacular, unbelievable and wonderful applied to events, people, circumstances and experiences that were "schlecht" (not so good)? Even our German word for extremely good is now the household term for a ride-sharing car company, Uber. These hyped-up words that could be breaking open real feelings of real wonder fall on your ears evoking no feeling at all. Perhaps you have been fooled too many times. You are being quickly impoverished in a sea of confused, jacked-up terminology that is disconnected from the real feelings they were once representing. So how can this be turned around? How do you recover your wonderment if the language you are using to express it is now so impotent?

"If I had influence with the good fairy... I should ask that her gift to each child in the world be a sense of wonder so indestructible that it would last throughout life."

-Rachel Carson

AGELESS TIP

LET YOUR INNOCENCE
WRITE A LOVE LETTER

TO YOU

Here are a few ideas to recover some actual feelings of wonderment and acquire a stronger foundation of learning. One is to write a love letter to yourself. Let the inner innocence of your heart speak to you. Take the time to listen without judgement. It may have been quite some time, so be patient. Write down the messages and come back to them in a few weeks. Make it a monthly practice. This will help you stay in touch with your heart and your tender, innocent nature.

Accepting the possibility that your "socially constructed reality" is absorbing your energy completely is a good step as well. Heal your all-consuming fascination sickness. Just the realization that no energy is available to you for the experience of wonderment can serve as a much needed wake-up call.

Additionally you might consider the possibility that your experience of wonder lies outside the "constructed social reality" and cannot be entered into from that doorway. Once that possibility is absorbed, a third way may present itself to you. You, yourself, without any "cultural" interference or conditioning have always had access to the springs of joyful wonderment. All through your life nothing has ever been in the way of this experience except what you agreed to place there yourself. In order to stay inside the "socially conditioned reality" you may have paid a high price.

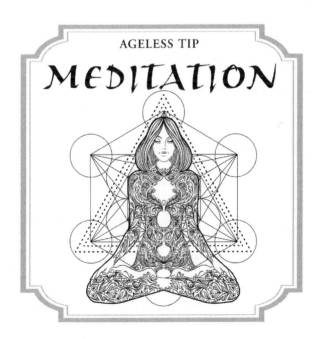

AGELESS TIP

MEDITATION

"The art of meditation is a way of getting into touch with reality, and the reason for it is that most civilized people are out of touch with reality because they confuse the world as it is with the world as they think about it and talk about it and describe it."　　~ Alan Watts

The world as it is and what you "think about it" are not the same thing. The simple act of giving your attention to your present experience, without judgement is the essence of being mindful and can unlock a direct perception of the world "as it is." The challenge for you is to sustain your attention in the present and not wander off into your judgements. The practice of staying present is essential to recover and strengthen the vitality of your lifelong learning adventure. Your resilience is one of the characteristics of all lifelong learners. This is a theme of special interest to Thomas Hübl, my Austrian spiritual teacher. Since 2004 Thomas has been active worldwide, organizing talks, workshops, trainings, tonings and larger events such as the popular Celebrate Life Festival held annually in Germany. He taught me to practice meditation in a way that takes me into more blissful and expansive states of awakening while also leading me to be more grounded, available and effective in the world.

*"Once we dive deeper, then we become
like a laser, a laser that penetrates every level of
reality and goes deeper and deeper and deeper until
finally, wherever you look, you just see the
authentic evolutionary impulse working every
moment - fresh."*

~ Thomas Hübl

SEE WITH FRESH EYES!

It is through your ability to sustain viewing
yourself and others with fresh eyes that you can experience
the real magic of life as it unfolds moment to moment. With
practice you can expand your conscious capacity for higher
insight, communion and realization while at the same time
navigate daily life with increased presence, focus and clarity.
Create a space which repeatedly will enable a deepening of
your own presence, transparency, compassion and ability to
express yourself authentically. I also learned from him to
question whether the way I interpret my life and reality is

still appropriate. He led me to deeper levels of self-understanding and personal responsibility.

DON"T BELIEVE IT!
"TOO OLD" IS JUST AN IDEA
THAT HAS NO POWER OVER YOU.

In shaking off your cultural "aging beliefs" and setting for yourself the challenge of shaping a new culture, you need to learn to focus your attention. Establishing and maintaining daily practices of mindfulness and meditation can radically restore and sustain the feeling of the wonder of your life. There are many tools that you can use to create environments for yourself to support the feeling of wonderment. You can design a sacred space in your home or find an inspiring location where you feel uplifted. You can create a selection of music that supports the quality of wonder that opens you the most effectively. There are many short films that are powerful guides to facilitate a deep dive into the wonderment of what and who you are. Use them continually to loosen the grip of your "socially constructed reality." I have a few films linked on my website that I use and I recommend them for your use as well. Use whatever tools you wish to shape a supportive environment and then engage sustained mindful and meditative practices to gain more direct access to your felt sense of wonder. This feeling, as it grows and matures in you, will form a life-giving foundation for all your future education and learning.

www.agelessthebook.com/wonderment

"Until one is committed,
there is hesitancy, the chance to draw back —
concerning all acts of initiative (and creation),
there is one elementary truth that ignorance of
which kills countless ideas and splendid plans: that
the moment one definitely commits oneself, then
Providence moves too.

All sorts of things occur to help one that would
never otherwise have occurred. A whole stream of
events issues from the decision, raising in one's
favor all manner of unforeseen incidents and
meetings and material assistance, which no man
could have dreamed would have come his way.

Whatever you can do,
or dream you can do, begin it.
Boldness has genius, power,
and magic in it. Begin it now."

~ Goethe

AN AGELESS LIVING FUTURE

A vibrant human being, an attractive human being, is an engaging and evolving participant in life. To be on the sidelines of life, watching at a safe distance, is a sure way to stay safe, but at what cost? Your true vibrancy and beauty will be a hidden and buried treasure. Eventually it may be hidden even to you and its value lost forever. Don't let that be your destiny. Engage fully in your present life and commit to evolve with a firm resolve.

"An amazing thing happens when you stop seeking approval and validation: You find it. People are naturally drawn like magnets to those who know who they are and cannot be shaken!"
~Mandy Hale, *The Single Woman*

To be stepping out of the current aging paradigm there has to be clear understanding of what you are stepping into. It's not enough to say "No" to the conservative and established models of aging. You also need to provide, plant and nurture the new ideas, restore joyful learning methods, build appropriate health and wellness models, and most of all bring into focus the vision of a new future for yourself and your communities. Take time to imagine a thriving future for yourself in the decades to come. Write down the details of your future self and future life. Review and update them regularly. Explore new kinds of knowing. Expand.

THE NEW **CULTURE OF AGELESS LIVING** WILL
TRANSFORM OUR IDEAS ABOUT EDUCATION
RADICALLY!

MANY KINDS OF INTELLIGENCE

The theory of multiple intelligences challenges the idea of a single IQ, in which you have one central "computer" where intelligence is housed. Howard Gardner, the Harvard professor who originally proposed the theory, says that there are multiple types of human intelligence, each representing different ways of processing information:

- Verbal-linguistic intelligence
- Logical-mathematical intelligence
- Visual-spatial intelligence
- Musical intelligence
- Naturalistic intelligence
- Bodily-kinesthetic intelligence
- Inter-personal intelligence
- Intra-personal intelligence

The reason this theory is so vitally important to the Ageless Living revolution is that a broader definition of what a human being is needs to be accompanied by a broader definition of the kinds of intelligence that can and will be expanded. In this theory of multiple intelligences, many types of intelligence coexist and reveal a rich extension of the narrow ideals of high IQ's.

I believe extending your education in the long life you are living will be a source not only of personal enjoyment, but will also mold a new world for you that will hold more diverse artistic expressions and other cultural riches.

Personal vibrancy and attractiveness arise in the quality of your relationship with life. This relationship may be best represented as a dance. Life is moving and you are moving. If you think of life as the music you are moving to, composing and conducting and you as a dancer, you can see that when the two are in dynamic harmony and move together, a vibrant "presence" is possible.

AGELESS

"In Hinduism, Shiva the Cosmic Dancer, is perhaps the most perfect personification of the dynamic universe. Through his dance, Shiva sustains the manifold phenomena in the world, unifying all things by immersing them in his rhythm and making them participate in the dance - a magnificent image of the dynamic unity of the Universe."

~ Fritjof Capra

Learning is also about seeing with more sensitivity. Through the ages we have refined our senses to pick up more than the outer aspects of people. Jane Austen writes in Sense and Sensibility:

"At first sight, his address is certainly not striking; and his person can hardly be called handsome, till the expression of his eyes, which are uncommonly good, and the general sweetness of his countenance, is perceived."

The dance you are living is not pre-programmed to slowly and painfully come to an end, diminishing and fading day by day. Esther (Abraham) Hicks has often said that the idea that you have to go through a slow and often painful or debilitating decline as you mature is not at all how it has to be. She states in a number of her talks that this is how it can be for you:

"Happy - Healthy,
Happy- Healthy,
Happy - Healthy
- Dead!"

"This is the real secret of life – to be completely engaged with what you are doing in the here and now. And instead of calling it work, realize it is play."

Alan Watts, British philosopher and writer

Ageless Tip

BE BOLD!

Streams
of events
will issue
from your
decisions.

SELF-WORTH AND SELF-CARE

Stories of aging are everywhere in our society. They are in the films we watch, the TV series we consume, the books we read, the conversations we have and most importantly they are inside us. Stories of aging live in your conscious mind, your subconscious mind and are embedded in your body. These stories hold many beliefs, perceptions and convey vivid experiences that serve as role models in your ideas about aging. The stories may be holding indirect messages about aging that are woven into plot lines. Whatever shape they may take, be aware that every story is full of "signals" that are creating a culture of aging within you as well as around you. This culture has a history and is shaping your present day beliefs, attitudes and actions. It also plays a role in your future expectations. The current culture of aging has woven together thousands of stories to form an understanding of aging that now lives inside you and billions of other human beings.

In writing new stories about yourself that will free you from this aging culture it is vital to understand the relationship between self-worth and self-care. This relationship is important to understand for two reasons. The first is that only with strong self-worth will your commitment to self-care be strong. The second is that self-worth and self-care enhance and support each other. This story of your worth and the care you show yourself colors profoundly your history and your plans for the future. We are all storytellers, weaving meaning into the activities of our lives. Without your stories your daily activities are not infused with power and depth that the way they could be.

Your ageless lifestyle needs a plan. The plan is created and held in writing new, vibrant stories that define you as you choose to be defined. No longer complying with the cultural "messages," you are standing up with courage and replacing them with new affirmations. You will be recalling and recovering some of the stories you have been holding to. And most importantly you are exposing the vital relationship that has always played out in your life between your self-worth and your purpose.

"Health and longevity studies show that when people live with a sense of purpose, no matter how big or small, they live longer and happier lives."
~Marci Shimoff, Happy for No Reason

ALISON'S STORY

Alison heard me talking about the importance of skin care specifically for mature skin and the uplifting effects it has on self esteem at a business presentation. It took her almost two years to pick up the phone and make a consultation appointment with me. She arrived at my office with no energy, her face lifeless and grey, she weighed 30 pounds over her normal weight and on top of that, she was depressed. "Look at me, I am old and I feel it," she said. "My husband is cheating on me and I am so tired. Is there anything you can do for my old skin?"

I asked her age. She was six years younger than me. I didn't share my own age with her at that time. I put her in my air pressure machine, which stimulates the lymphatic circulation, and helped her body detoxify. Meanwhile I peeled the grey layer of dead cells off of her face and customized a treatment for her skin rejuvenation. I doubled her moisture level and sealed it into her skin. Now she would be able to keep that glowing complexion for weeks by using specific skin care products I recommended to her. I handed her a mirror, she was literally speechless looking at her transformed face. That lifeless, sad, desperate "old" lady sprang up and went straight to a larger mirror. "I can't believe this is my face. I look ten years younger." She turned around, tears rolling down her face, "How did you do that?" she asked. "How could you make me so much younger looking?"

I then shared my age with her and she stared at me in total disbelief. "I want what you have, please teach me what you are doing. I want your energy, your body shape, your happiness, and zest for life. I want to bring all my friends to experience this as well." She wanted to party to show off her face. It was one of these touching transformational moments I experience almost daily which make my professional life so rewarding. I saw a different woman with a new perspective in front of me. Her energy and smiles were lighting up the room. At that moment she didn't think that she was "old" or ugly. She had finally taken the time to make self-care her first priority. She felt instantly beautiful and younger looking. She had transformed before my eyes. With just one single visit, her self-esteem had restored her joyful energy. "What would your husband think about this new vivacious woman coming home and maybe enticing him to dance with you?" I said.

During her third visit she shared with me her newly revived romance with her husband. Even I couldn't

believe that she was that same depressed Alison from three months earlier. She felt beautiful and found her self-worth. She had changed her beliefs about aging and no longer felt old and ugly. My newly developed product line was working wonders for her prematurely aged skin. She was more than impressed with the way her skin returned to a flawless glow over the short period of three months.
Alison's world had shifted into agelessness.

In the next chapter the role and significance of the story you tell yourself about your value and worth in your is explored. The value you give to your own being will determine your destiny in every area of your ageless life. Remember that you are perfectly made and are valuable beyond measure. If you desire a rich and beautiful destiny you must value yourself as rich and beautiful. Remember this every day and hold fast to this key to your miraculous life at any age. And when you help others remember that they too are perfectly made and are valuable beyond measure, you will be doubly blessed.

Chapter 7

YOUR SELF-WORTH
STORY

You have a story of self-worth you tell yourself. Everyone has this story. It is made up of many statements, impressions, actions and fabrications. This individual story of your unique value is shaping your beliefs, perceptions and experiences today. Here are a few exercises to discover for yourself what makes up the content of your own personal self-worth story. How you felt about this content and what conclusions you came to during the three main stages of life are major elements in the tale.

I invite you to examine and re-write the content, emotional quality and purpose of your self-worth. The values and experiences from your childhood, youth and adulthood are each valuable and contributed to the layering and richness of your character. Identifying these layers will help clarify how you arrived at the sense of personal worth you experience today and will offer you choices to keep what is still useful and meaningful and to let go of those beliefs and values that are no longer in alignment with your current life.

Write down the answers to these questions:

SELF-WORTH

1. **What were you told about your worth in early childhood?**

   _____

   _____

   _____

2. What actions of your family shaped the quality of self-worth you felt?

   _____

   _____

   _____

3. How did you feel about these statements or actions?

   _____

   _____

   _____

4. What conclusions did you come to about your self-worth?

   _____

   _____

   _____

5. What were you told about your worth in your teenage years?

6. What actions of your friends and family shaped the quality of self-worth you felt?

7. How did you feel about these statements or actions?

8. What conclusions did you come to about your self-worth?

9. What were you told about your worth in your adult years?

10. What actions of your friends and family shaped the quality of self-worth you felt?

_____

_____

_____

11. How did you feel about those statements or actions?

_____

_____

_____

12. What conclusions did you come to about your self-worth?

_____

_____

_____

13. Are there any you wish to keep? Any to let go of?

_____

_____

_____

_____

14. **What would you like to add now to your sense of self-worth?**

_____

_____

_____

YOUR SELF-CARE STORY

Self-care in the light of ageless living is an expression of your autonomy and your character. It is not the opposite of being cared for by "professional" care providers who attend, predominately, to the needs of the body exclusively. This clinical definition of "self-care" has long outworn its usefulness in attempting to clarify the term. If you remain enthralled by this description you will remain stagnating in the mediocre vision of a body-centered care regimen that has nothing to offer the your character and your soul.

Obviously our challenge lies in the scope of the word "self." Self as body, self as mind, self as spirit are three aspects of self. When integrated in the holistic world-view they can be referred to as the Body/Mind. So self-care, as I am presenting it, is Body/Mind care that is self directed, purposeful, progressive, evolutionary, flexible, intuitive, disciplined and aimed at supporting your sense of self-worth and the force of your character. Valuing self-care is holding a vision of your body/mind as a dynamic being; expanding, contracting, growing, shedding, embodied, transcendent and rich in mystery, subtlety, diversity and complexity. The dynamic nature of your body/mind means constant changes are arising. These changes require your attention, maintenance, nourishment, cleansing, transporting, returning, collecting, assessing and many other "caring" activities.

SELF-ESTEEM ISN'T EVERYTHING; IT'S JUST
THAT THERE'S NOTHING WITHOUT IT.

~ Gloria Steinem

Self-care is a character trait that, when practiced
well, gives you a foundation of wellness that is responsive
and fluid. It changes as your needs change. It holds only
those practices that currently serve and seeks out new
practices to serve the coming needs that your imagination
dreams into being. I see this kind of self-care being regard as
an art. It will taught as an art. When seen in an
accomplished person, he or she will be regarded as a master
of the art. There will be specialized areas of this art serving
aspects of human powers not yet visible.

> *"No matter how much effort is exhausted, the
> goal of acting in a heart-centered way does not
> occur on a regular basis when your nervous system
> is overstimulated.*
>
> *This is why unraveling the overstimulated
> nervous system in the most loving manner is the
> central theme of the new spiritual paradigm."*
>
> ~ Matt Khan, *Whatever Arises, Love That*

This kind of artistic self-care is also based on honesty. The kind of honesty that embraces the fullness of your character. Supplying what you need to engage in self-actualization, self-transcendence and mindful embodiment is the role of this art. As for its execution, like all arts it will involve your imagination, design, practice, implementation and evaluation. You are the canvas and the painter in this art. Self-care and self-creation will go hand in hand in your ageless living revolution. No motivational lectures will be required if you value it highly enough.

In the light of this broader definition of your self-care I invite you to examine and re-write your self-care story. The values and experiences from your childhood, youth and adulthood are each valuable and contributed to the layering and richness of your character.

Write down the answers to these questions concerning what went into and formed your sense of self-care. Pay attention to how this changed over the stages of your life.

SELF-CARE

1. **What were you told about your self-care in early childhood?**

2. What actions of my family shaped the quality of self-care I felt and practiced?

3. How did you feel about these statements or actions?

4. What conclusions did you come to about your self-care?

5. **What were you told about your self-care in your teenage years?**

6. What actions of your family or friends shaped the quality of self-care you felt and practiced?

7. How did I feel about these statements or actions?

8. What conclusions did you come to about your self-care?

9. **What were you told about your self-care in your adult years?**

10. What actions from my friends and family contributed to the quality of self-care you felt and practiced?

11. How did you feel about these statements or actions?

12. What conclusions did you come to about your self-care?

_____

13. Are there any you wish to keep? Any to let go of?

_____

14. What would you like to add now to your sense of self-care?

_____

Discovering the many streams and rivers that flow into this vital area in your life can be revealing. For most of us there was not any logical sequence or coherent structure that we can point to and say, "my self-worth is constructed of these 5 things or came into it's present state on a specific date." It is too complex, and much of the foundation was put in place in the preverbal stages of our lives, making it even more elusive to express with thoughts. There is also a real danger living in situations in which your sense of worth is assaulted in blatant or subtle ways on a continual basis. After a while people tend to push away the assaults, hits and shocks to their self-esteem and lock them away. This can only solve the problem in a "survival" mode and takes a tremendous toll on our long term well-being. The scenario that all too often plays out is like that of a time traveler. One day the person who has seemingly "overcome" all the hits finds themselves not recognizing the person looking back at them from the bathroom mirror. This shock, this "What has happened to me?" bursts the bubble of denial and can start the process of the real recovery of a healthy self-worth.

CREATING A NEW SELF-WORTH STORY

In India, when a master teacher is about to engage a disciple in rigorous spiritual practice that will dismantle much of the student's current egoic structures and self beliefs, the master will often find it necessary to first strengthen the student's self-worth. The foundation of the student is fortified around three themes. The aspirant is instructed in their Divine origin, his or her noble nature, and their glorious destiny. Once strengthened, the master will proceed, knowing full well that the disciple would likely not remain in the training without a strong foundation of self-worth.

Creating a new story about your self-worth can be life-changing, and can result in practices of self-care that accelerate those changes in unexpected ways. One of the gifts of being human is the gift of free will. You can use this freedom to enhance your life by creating a story of self-worth that truly inspires your mind and heart. Now you understand that many elements have been combined to form your sense of self-worth and self-care. You have composed a story about who you are. Left unchanged, this will continue to play out and color everything you experience. If you choose to change your story and write a new one, new skills will be needed. You need skills you can practice and master that support the art of creating a personal story of your unique self-worth.

"Practice means to perform, over and over again in the face of all obstacles, some act of vision, of faith, of desire. Practice is a means of inviting the perfection desired."

~ Martha Graham

What is a self-worth story? What are the things that need to be in your story? Core beliefs, emotions, perspectives, affirmations, cooperations and commands are a few things to consider including. Here is an example of an affirmative self-worth story.

I am worthy of life and trust my commitment in this. I am worthy of love and trust my commitment in this. I am worthy of self-reflection and mindfulness and trust my commitment to this. I am worthy of being supported and supporting others and trust my commitment in this. I am worthy to determine and execute my plans and trust my commitment in this.

What is your self-care story? What things need to be in your story? Core beliefs, emotions, perspectives, affirmations, cooperations and commands are again a few things to consider including.

I practice self-care in my life and trust my ability in this. I practice self-care for my power to love and trust my ability to commit to this. I practice self-care of my mindfulness and trust my abilities in this. I practice self-care of my own supportive nature and my support of others and trust my ability in this. I practice self-care to nurture my determination and execution of my plans and trust my abilities in this. I practice self-care towards all areas of my body/mind.

Your health of your self-care rests upon the foundation of your healthy story of self-worth. The new ageless life you create for yourself requires that you spend time expanding and enriching your foundation of self-worth. Any rushing over this vital step will weaken, in turn, the needed self-care practices that will ensure your ongoing vitality of body, mind and spirit.

SELF-CORRECTION AND NEGATIVE SELF TALK

Any plan you set in motion should have clear goals so that your actions can be aligned and move you in the direction you choose for yourself. There is, however, one more skill you will need to support ageless living and that is the ability to self-correct. Making small decisions that bring you back on course if you stray off is self-correction. This is a core discipline. In practice it is micro discipline. Your practice of this skill will reduce the negative self-talk and strengthen your self-worth. You are always faced with two choices in moving ahead with your plans. You choose discipline or you choose regret. So choose discipline every time and no regret will be able to poison you. Also know that many of the masters of business, art, science and education are "off course" 90+% of the time, but are self-correcting again and again in a never ending pattern that ultimately lands them exactly inside the goals they have set.

> NEW BELIEFS WILL
> UNLOCK NEW HUMAN POTENTIAL

Ageless living with healthy self-worth is also supported by having high mental and physical functioning, having low risks of disease and being engaged in life. These come together in artistic activities. Art in its various modes, visual, musical, theatrical all promote a vital engagement in your life. They keep you positively involved and healthy in fulfilling ways. Quality of life is much more of a "motivator" to exercise and eat healthy foods than dry lectures and to-do lists. When you are taught to view exercise as a kind of "medicine" that you should do for some future benefit, you are much less likely to make it a priority. Many studies are now confirming that there is a "branding problem" when it comes to how most people think about exercise.

"I'm seeing more and more clients who stay home and don't get out and are spending hours in front of the television. Their health deteriorates at an alarming rate compared to someone who actually is getting out to the senior citizen centers or participating in community-based exercise programs. The health benefits of elder patients becoming physically active are multifaceted," says Karen Ross, MD, an assistant professor at the University of Oklahoma Health Sciences Center.

SOUND MINDS IN SOUND BODIES

There is, of course an abundance of information available to us on staying physically healthy. Often we look for the latest finding or the most current study to fulfill our insatiable curiosity. The history of our collective fascination with health is long and varied. The high standard set by the early Greeks of sound minds in sound bodies was revived by the famed Italian educator, Vittorino da Feltre, the first to balance physical and mental training in the 14th century. Here in America a colorful cast of trainers, authors and even celebrities have contributed their insights, stories and practices over the last hundred years. The first of these colorful personalities in the US appeared in the early 20th Century. Bernard MacFadden was known as the father of physical culture. In 1915 he wrote:

> "Inactivity is non-existence. It means death. Our bodily powers and organs were given to us for a definite purpose. Failure to use them brings serious penalties. There can be no health, no real health, with physical stagnation."

Over one hundred years later this simple message has yet to be assimilated and implemented by the majority of Americans. Why is this? Many of his other councils, such as keeping our sports activities playful, our exercise regimens joyful and eating slowly with enjoyment are essential to our health. Again and again did he steer us to be active with "joyful" movement. He set the tone and the pattern for many who followed in his path to help awaken in you the desire for physical excellence.

A sedentary lifestyle is surely not going to lead you or anyone to ageless living. Vitality is essential, and it is found in moving every day with joy.

CREATIVITY AND THE ARTS

So what does motivate us to move, dance, swim, climb, run, lift weights, ski, play sports and engage in actions other than sitting home. Quality of life is what motivates us. Creating quality of life is a universal passion. Participating in some creative activity is deeply woven into what it means to be human. "You do not need anybody's permission to live a creative life," Elizabeth Gilbert writes, in her book, *Big Magic: Creative Living Beyond Fear.* She makes a powerful case for committing to participate with your creative nature, realize its depth, it's magical nature and stand humbly in the presence of inspiration. She also adds: "If you're alive, you're a creative person. You and I and everyone you know are descended from tens of thousands of years of makers. Decorators, tinkerers, storytellers, dancers, explorers, fiddlers, drummers, builders, growers, problem-solvers, and embellishers—these are our common ancestors."

Many benefits are found in engaging in art activities. Some of these are:

- Supporting a more meaningful sense of your self-esteem
- Improving your thinking and overall brain function
- Enhancing your social life
- Helping you relax
- Providing you a sense of control
- Reducing your anxiety and depression
- Stimulating your playfulness
- Engendering your sense of humor

- Increasing your multi-sensory stimulation
- Fostering in you a renewed and stronger sense of identity
- Nurturing your spirituality

One of the most difficult situations faced by many people in our society is isolation. To be isolated and to be elderly is extremely challenging. Expressive, artistic activities can lessen or remove altogether this damaging and depressing situation. The arts also support the healing and restorative powers of self-expression and can greatly improve communication skills.

THE ARTS PROVIDE ENDLESS OPPORTUNITIES TO ENGAGE WITH OTHERS CREATIVELY

REVIVAL OF THE ARTS

The ageless living revolution will see a tremendous revival of the arts. The commodity rich, spiritually bankrupt society that offers readymade everything is being exposed as a shallow counterfeit of real human culture. If we do not make things, but only consume them, we are out of step with human happiness. I foresee a revolution coming that will reverse the trend toward acquiring ever more lifeless things. Things, clothing, jewelry and furniture that are entirely anonymous are devoid of a deeper significance to you because you have no idea of who made them, why they made them, how they came to you. These endless things are already starting to lose their spell and addictive power over you. You will want to make things again. You will make them because you enjoy making things. You will once again want to live in rooms that "speak" to you. You will want to know the story of the chair you sit in and its maker. You will tell the tale of the seamstress and the path taken to create the dress or suit you wear.

Having millions of Chinese sit in warehouse factories making countless lifeless objects for people they will never meet is robbing the human race of a fundamental happiness. The simple joy of connecting with the human being who made something you use or wear is a meaningful human act. Looking them in the eye, being able to express your appreciation of the thing they made and your appreciation of them will reconnect you again and again to the magic of your unique life.

I have a friend who, when he was living in New York City, began a lifelong habit of asking to meet the owners of the restaurants he dined in. He quickly learned that this was a very rare request. To his surprise every owner who was on the premises would emerge to greet him and thank him personally for asking to meet. They sometimes would share the stories of their beginnings and felt seen and proud of what they had created. Upon returning to dine after those meetings my friend found his experiences were very different. Often the owner would come out to greet him, and, if near to closing time, would invite him to stay and enjoy himself even as the other guests took their leave. I was with him recently and saw this for myself. Stopping by our table, the owner shared with me the fascinating and dramatic tale of how she came to America, how through the miraculous generosity of a friend she was able to acquire the beautiful restaurant we were sitting in. I left stunned at the richness of our lunch and how this simple relationship transformed my experience as well.

Now and then I too will inquire to meet the owner of a shop or restaurant. I personally thank them and compliment them on their efforts. I listen to them and feel their pride. My connection to the place, to them and to myself is transformed. It loses the feeling of just another business establishment and shines with a uniqueness that is rich with the feeling, commitment and efforts of another human being. This face to face, eye to eye encounter is a fundamental human activity that is woven deep into our love of belonging and relating.

> *"To consciously evolve, we require clear vision of a compassionate future that draws out our enthusiastic participation in life."*
>
> ~ *Duane Elgin,* American author, speaker, consultant, and media activist.

In mastering your ageless living lifestyle, a healthy sense of self-worth along with good self-care practices will support the transition out of your current aging paradigm. Implementing micro self-correction as a daily discipline will minimize any undermining your self worth by preventing regret, self-criticism and negative self-talk. Have a plan to guide your progress and set the end goals clearly. Create a new model, recite new stories and participate heartily in living a self-directed, happy, healthy and abundant life. In these ways you can live free of the "culture of aging" for the rest of your miraculous life.

Visit my website to learn about my Ageless Living Wealth Academies. In these you can learn more about the role self-worth and the arts in agelessness, and experience with others the transforming power of turning back the "aging clock."

Chapter 8

MY EARLY YEARS
AND TRAINING

POSTWAR GERMANY

I grew up in Hameln, near Hannover, Germany. It is a well-known town with its beautiful architecture preserved and restored over centuries and for the famous story, The Pied Piper of Hamlin. Each year during the summer, visitors enjoy watching the tragic tale about broken promises, trust and revenge from centuries ago which is still touching the hearts of many from around the world to this day.

I arrived on July 12, 1946 and I was a surprise for my parents. Our doctor had told my mom that she couldn't get pregnant unless she would have an operation. My dad refused any surgical intervention and said "If it's meant to be, we will have a child, if not, we will accept it. I won't let anybody mess with your body, period!" It was a great surprise to the doctor when I was conceived and arrived safely. All were thrilled.

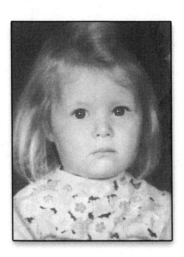

I still remember the many bombed out buildings around our home. Some had collapsed and others were riddled with bullet holes. At that time there were still many more horse carriages than cars. People had just enough to eat and most were very poor. We kids never felt poor though. Almost everyone grew their own fruits and veggies. We had every kind of healthy, naturally grown nutrition, food without any pesticides. I believe that laid the foundation for the healthy constitution I am still benefitting from to this day.

SPECIAL DELIVERY

My little sister Ingelore, was born about four years after me. Mom had prepared me for a little brother so I had a problem from the moment I laid my eyes on her. I had waited so long for "his" arrival, I even sacrificed my allowance of sugar cubes each week for the stork so he knew where to deliver him. After a girl was dropped off I waited angry and disappointed for that stork to pick her up, drop her back into the baby pond and exchange her for the right baby - my brother. Finally, overshadowed with disappointment, I had to deal with her not being "returned." To this day, we have never developed a loving relationship.

Despite our challenges we had some wonderful childhood times, playing outdoors throughout the seasons from spring to winter enjoying all the magic. Dad built a little cottage in our garden, where we would spend weekends grilling and preparing veggies and fruits we harvested right there. Sometimes we visited my favorite Aunt Berta who lived an hour drive away from us. She had more fruit and berries than we, making it such a joy to pick and eat as much as we liked. We used to walk for endless miles through forests and meadows singing along the back country roads where we harvested cherries, pears and apples. It was such a magical time. We picked armfuls of flowers and wove beautiful wreaths for our heads.

We looked like little elves running thru the high spring grass. We chased the cows until they had enough of our playful teasing. The two of us squealed with excitement when they suddenly would turn around and chase us elves out of their meadows.

During my childhood, my dad was managing a huge company which was rebuilding and expanding the roads around northern Germany. It was founded by five brothers, and were one of the first companies that hired guest workers from Yugoslavia, Greece, Italy and Turkey. Needless to say, he had many challenges to deal with. Between the rival brothers, who were jealous of each other, and the foreigners who had still to deal with the stigmas of war, my dad was the ever watchful peacemaker paving a road of his own through some very rocky terrains. The workers loved my dad. Upon returning from their short vacations in their home countries, they brought an endless supply of their best cheeses, wines, hams and other delicacies to us. Even though the times were harsh and clashes were an ongoing problem, I saw a spirit of goodness and generosity that pervaded their hearts. Growing up in Germany opened my eyes to both the harshness of life and its loving-kindness and generosity.

MY EUROPEAN TRAINING

In the opening chapter I shared the circumstances and journeys that got me to Iran. Here I would like to share with you how it was I returned to Europe to be trained in a new career. The most modern and prestigious clinic for plastic surgery in the Middle East was being planned to be built just south of Tehran, and I was offered the position of the Spa Director. I was also enlisted to help design the facility. I was very excited about my first duty, which was to fly to the US and the UK to finalize the contracts with the pre-selected group of plastic surgeons. Arrangements were made for me to research and observe for one month at the Red Door Spa in Beverly Hills, and at the Guerlain Spa in St Moritz, Switzerland. The estimated time until completion of the project was about one year and six months.

I went back to Germany for six months to research more about the advancements in post-op healing, and to select and order the most advanced technical tools available. I went back to my former Aesthetic School in Cologne to brush up on the latest research and advancements in Aesthetics. John Herfs, the owner of the school, announced to me that he had just signed a contract with Switzerland to provide the first C.I.D.E.S.C.O education in Germany. (Comité International d'Esthétique et de Cosmétologie)

This organization was to provide the most prestigious and comprehensive education for Aestheticians who wanted to become the highest ranking, and having the highest paid positions in this field internationally. I asked my partners in Tehran for permission to stay in Germany and enroll in the training program. When that agreement came through, I registered myself immediately. I was one of the first students.

The rumors and signs of a revolution in Iran started to increase. One day my then twelve year old daughter cried on the phone from Iran "Mommy come back, I am so afraid; soldiers are shooting with tanks near our school and they set one of our busses on fire." I was so worried about her, but was quickly reassured that she was safe and well protected by the family and I could complete my education. Colette arrived safely on

December 10th, 1978 by British Airways in Cologne, Germany. We both had no idea that it was the last chance for her to leave Iran. Her dad was supposed to follow days later but was denied permission to board the plane. He remained in Iran and eventually passed away there.

I didn't know that the political revolution would change Iran so radically. I never imagined that I would not be able to return to Tehran. The Royal Family was forced to leave the country and the magic of those days, with all the beauty and splendor vanished forever. The Queen Mother left with her entourage and soon after passed away. The many palace visits and the royal train journey are forever etched in my heart. Her kindness, her protection and the love she expressed toward me spoke eloquently of the goodness of the Iranian culture, whose long history has enriched the world with its arts and sciences.

I completed my C.I.D.E.S.C.O. training over the next 18 months, followed by a six-month apprenticeship. I then received the prestigious C.I.D.E.C.S.O. Diplomat Certification Award, the highest honor bestowed in the field of Aesthetics.

NORTHERN CALIFORNIA

In 1987 I relocated to the United States and settled in Northern California. I remarried and found myself taking care of my new family for the first several years. My mother-in-law soon arrived from Tehran. She was fragile and required constant care. She had cancer and we all devoted ourselves to care for her. We never revealed to her how ill she actually was. The family did a great job assuring her that she soon would be better and return to her beloved home in Tehran. She never knew about her situation, helping me to have such wonderful time with her. The gratitude my mother-in-law displayed was so touching. We bonded deeply. I made her laugh and asked her very personal questions about her happiness and how it felt having been a woman in Iran all her life. She honored me by sharing her most personal feelings so openly. I could see how much she enjoyed speaking freely for the first time about herself. She asked me to never share these revelations with anyone and I promised.

One day before we left to visit a friend of hers, I asked for permission to apply lipstick and rouge on her cheeks. I fixed her hair nicely and we selected the nicest dress she owned. She looked into the mirror over and over again. Her happy smile was lighting up her face. She had transformed into more than a much younger version of herself. Her image more closely reflected her character, perhaps something of the playful beauty of her character. It was revealed and seen by her and by me. Tears of joy welled up in my eyes. The little "makeup ritual" was an act of self-care that deeply resonated with her, and energized her sense of self-worth. Her confidence in feeling that the inner beauty of her soul could be held in the image of her outer beauty was for that brief moment fully restored. I kissed her hands and we both giggled all way to her friend's residence. Upon opening the door to greet us, her friend was astounded and didn't recognize the women she had known all her life. She couldn't stop confiding to me how happy she was for her son to have found me after two failed marriages.

Eventually she flew with one of her daughters and granddaughter back home to Iran, where she died several weeks later. Once again I had seen a woman transform and shape shift into a restored version of their earlier appearance. Our spirits are powerful medicine and can bring about swift changes to our form, energy and force of character.

BUILDING MY SKIN CARE PRACTICE

After several years of adjusting to my new life in California, I wanted to get back into my passion as an Aesthetician. I opened the Dermatiq Day Spa in Danville. In 1994 I joined the Danville Chamber of Commerce, which tirelessly helped my new venture to become successful.

Education is a passion for me and I am known to be innovative and unique in my approach to skin care. I expanded into advanced therapy modalities that keep me and my clients agile, energetic, healthy and younger looking. My practice has been thriving now for twenty years.

My marriage eventually ended. We grew in very different directions. My personal life has undergone many big changes. One transforming experience after another has altered my life in the most profound and unexpected ways. My beliefs about life, people and what is possible have all expanded in ways I could never have anticipated. Among these changes was that my physical appearance, the very shape of my body, returned to its younger condition so dramatically. My experience was a revelation to me of what is possible when you shake off cultural beliefs and step up to claim a different view of life for yourself. We are starting a revolution of agelessness. Let's stop acting old. Let's dance with life and let's dance together in a new era of limitless possibilities.

MOVING AHEAD

With deep gratitude, I am moving ahead and committing myself to expanding my knowledge and capacity. I am striving to be a beacon of light. I am also committed to be a change agent, helping people understand that our lives and capacity will not diminish if we embrace the new paradigm of being independently Ageless. Let's take a mystical path in our lifetime by tapping into the hidden powers we have carried within us since conception. When we do, nothing will ever be the same.

I was listening this morning to Jean Houston speak about her own husband's transformation. He was in his 70's, wrinkled and tired and wanted to look and feel younger. That strong desire led him to allow Jean to put him through a short but powerful change in his perception and state of being. He agreed to be guided by her in also changing his diet and movement and in a few months he regained his good looks and vibrant energy. He recovered the appearance and energy of a forty-five year old. Both of them were elated.

I am so enthusiastic about what happens when you open your heart and soul to change. By breaking out of your emotional prison and setting yourself free the whole world will change. No one can do that for you but YOU. Let's learn and discover together and let's dance straight into heaven.

I revisited my past in writing this book and recalled many things I had almost forgotten over the years. This was sometimes accompanied by quite heavy outbursts of tears disrupting me in the short term, but helping me realize the blessings I have been receiving throughout the years. My life is vividly back now in my "memory treasure chest." Even the image of Trixie, one of the seven splendid peacocks I had raised, listening with her eyes closed to soft classical music in front of the radio in the living room was back. My peacock males with their full, colorful tails were spread before me time and time again. I raised them from baby peacocks to adults. I felt humbled and grateful to see their uniquely different characters develop and mature These are tender and beautiful stories for another time.

There was one more teacher in my life that I want to share with you. During the eight years we were together he was an example of how powerful a simple, devoted presence can be to heal, delight, teach and love. He never failed to surprise me with his enthusiasm and playfulness. Coming home to the top of the hill where our home was set, I was always greeted heartily by this friend. I often joined in sharing his unique and unusual language by answering his howling to greet him in return. He was a full-blooded timber wolf who had graciously accepted me as an alpha female and treated me with unusual respect. All I needed to do was to whisper that I didn't like certain behavior and he immediately put his head down and laid right next to me, his eyes asking for forgiveness. Initially, I was afraid he would harm my two cats. That proved not to be the case. He sensed they were "family" and honored my fondness for them. On many afternoons I would find him napping on our couch and there were the cats sleeping right beside him. Wolves are so smart. We share this world with so many marvelous creatures. I really want to teach children not to demonize wolves. These beings are magnificent and highly intelligent. Niki will be the well-known hero in one of my upcoming books.

    Your teachers will come in many forms. Some as friends and some as enemies. Each will spur on some aspect of your growth that needs to unfold. I encourage to not judge the forms these teachers will take. That which is hidden in you, ready to be born, is being nourished by mysterious allies and guides who know, far better than you, what is needed to aid your progress. Trust in life and embrace the good and the challenging.

    I have a fire burning in my soul now. I am getting to meet the woman in me whom I had lost touch with and who deeply touches me now. I am emotional as I recover her story, my story. My struggles with never feeling adequate, never good enough, not anyone special, echoing throughout my life had held me hostage. Now I see that after almost 70 long years of running away from those nightmares, I could have just stopped and confronted them and released them into the universe. I have discovered my rock-solid strength and power which I carried within me all along. The wise decisions I made even in the most dire situations where my life was endangered leave me today in awe. My journey has been a path of remembering and recovering the powers of my true nature.

MY RINGSIDE SEAT

Working with women from all walks of life, my business blessed me with a ringside seat to more tales of woe and joy than many busy psychotherapists hear. These stories have had one great theme run through them; "I do not want to age. I do not want to look old. I do not want to feel tired." I don't need a degree in psychotherapy to figure out that something is wrong here. It is deep and it is unsettling.

By having become the confidant to most of my clients, I have been honored by them to witness their deepest concerns and hopes. What is so glaringly missing is the understanding that "aging" as they are experiencing it is a cultural construct. They accept, as an unquestioned truth, that aging is an inevitable downward journey. This leads directly to their conformity with the cultural story. I invite you to question that story in all its forms and, in defiance, join me in a revolution that will undo the hold this aging story has on you. If you do you will open up a new chapter in your life that is written by your own hand. You will shape your own beliefs. You will set your own new goals. You will astound the world by achieving what now seems impossible. It is my joy to help you to ease your frustration and become your guide as you sculpt the character needed to ignite your own ageless living revolution.

In the following chapter I share with you some insights about beauty and health from my many years in the skin care industry. Be sure to visit my website. I am sharing in my blog, or as I like to call it, my journal, new technologies, best practices, tips and live events.

Chapter 9

THE VITALITY OF YOUR SKIN

Your face has a history and has unique needs to bring out its beauty. The art of skin care is all about the right sequence of treatments that match those needs. Once you experience the benefits of a well-designed self-care regimen, your skin, as well as your whole body, can restore itself to great health, regain astonishing vitality and preserve your beauty. Adopting a new practice of immaculate and sustained self-care takes determination. If you are willing to go the extra mile, learning to tune in and listen to your miraculous body when it lets you know what it needs, you can stay strong and pain free. You will look forward to live many more years with great joy and energy. I am the living proof of it.

HOW THE SKIN AGES

There are two issues regarding the aging of our skin. The belief that the skin is genetically programmed to age is false. The belief that aging skin is the result of it simply getting old because of the passage of time is also false. Regarding the timing of aging, Aubrey de Grey has stated,

'There is no ticking time bomb, just the accumulation of damage. Aging of the body, just like the aging of a car or a house, is merely a maintenance problem. And of course, we have hundred year old cars and (in Europe anyway), thousand-year-old buildings still functioning as well as when they were built, despite the fact that they were not designed to last even a fraction of that length of time. At the very least, the precedent of cars and houses gives us cause for cautious optimism that aging can be postponed indefinitely by sufficiently thorough and frequent maintenance."

Dramatically postponing aging is now possible with new scientific research swiftly unfolding, and the lifespans of human beings will most likely be extended well beyond the current assumptions of what is possible. What is being discussed here, of course, is purely a physiological matter with no concern for our faces as "images" of our character. The beautiful and richly detailed records of an accumulation of experiences, dreams, losses and triumphs that over time appear in a human face will still be "seen." They will simply be seen in a well-maintained and healthy face and body. Our faces hold so much of our character and are capable of radiating the richness of our dreams, accomplishments, hopes, fears and passions. Our face is our unique signature in this world. How many times have we heard, "I forget names all the time, but I never forget a face."

Skin aging and the changes it brings to your face has two separate effects. One is purely physical, but the other, the psychological effect can swiftly cascade into many degenerating and seemingly unrelated conditions. Seeing your face in a negative light can cause fear, loss of self-worth, loss of hope. These can trigger many other changes in your body, which further age you prematurely.

Skin is the largest of your beautiful organs. This "finest of clothing made," on average, weighs about 8 pounds (3.6 kilograms) and is elegantly wrapping you in 22 square feet (2 square meters) of living material. As we learned earlier, stress can be both good and bad. The damaging stress, intense or prolonged stress, can cause you mental tension and may result in harming your vascular system, raising your blood sugar levels, increasing your heart rate and blood pressure. This stress can be one of the most damaging enemies to our longevity. It can disrupt the many sets of biochemical and hormonal responses which begin in your brain and go on to affect your skin and the rest of your magnificent body. You have a great chance, if you adopt a truly healthy lifestyle, choose organic foods, drink plenty of water and most of all, commit to regular exercise to offset any stressors and damaging environmental effects. By improving the quality of your life, you will stay younger and energetic for many, many years to come.

You need to take the right steps for your body's overall maintenance and its long term care. The dangers of dehydration for example are far more severe than most of us realize. The vast majority of my clients are dehydrated, and I am not yet seeing this pattern change, despite my educating them about water. Dehydration symptoms start first with headaches and dryness in the mouth before they become more serious. Symptoms can include fatigue, dark-colored urine, confusion, dizziness, and chest pain. I recommend my clients to replenish water immediately after each bathroom visit. You can easily keep track of the right water level by checking the urine color. If it's almost colorless and has no odor to it, you are on the right track and every organ and cell in the body can function perfectly to keep you healthy.

Our actions are flowing from our beliefs and values. I strongly encourage you to value water more highly. The important role it is playing in your ageless life is worth examining in depth. Take the time to educate yourself and then create daily rituals, colorful reminders and love notes. Create records to track your progress. Improving this one aspect of your life can have far reaching consequences. Keep it fun and playful. Water is way more than we have been told. It has energetic properties, memories and every year more of it's mysterious nature is coming to light. Celebrate it every day!

Ageless Tip

WATER RITUAL

Drink 8 glasses of pure spring water each day.

"What spirit is so empty and blind,
that it cannot recognize the fact
that the foot is more noble than the shoe,
and skin more beautiful than the garment
with which it is clothed?"
~ Michelangelo

THE INTELLIGENCE OF YOUR SKIN

Even though skin acts to waterproof you and provide an insulating shield, guarding your body against extremes of temperature, damaging sunlight and harmful chemicals, it *thinks* as well. Your skin is a huge, living sensor, packed with millions and millions of nerves cells keeping you in touch with the outside world. Skin also is its own laboratory. It is creating Vitamin D from sunlight and providing this to the body to transform calcium into healthy bones. At the same time, skin grants you free movement, allowing you to be a single entity in the various environments you participate in. When needed it shields you like armor, but when no need is there for protection, it provides you with the loving intimacy of your sense of pressure and sensitive touch that is nothing short of miraculous. So don't take this beautiful "home of your heart and soul" for granted.

As a woman I think of my skin as the most precious dress I've ever owned. How beautiful do I look and feel in it, and how careful I am to preserve and cherish it. I invite you to reconsider what your skin is for you. This unique dress, this finest of clothing was created in the early stages of your life, before you even entered this world. It plays an essential role in your health and well being.

IN CONVERSATION

Women and men compliment me on my beautiful glowing complexion and that, of course, is a great conversation point. I then have an opportunity to share my field of expertise. Often women within hearing range join the conversation and I am happy, to share my insights. I usually keep the revelation of my age till the very last. The surprise and disbelief on their faces is uplifting and I would like every woman to experience this joy for herself. It just completely erases the "aging issue" for good. How invigorating it feels to be complimented on your skin when you are in your 60's, 70's and even 80's.

There is a difference when you are in your prime and receive compliments because you know how much time, money and effort you are putting into your appearance. Do you take these compliments for granted? It is a far more joyful experience when we, as mature women, receive compliments. Trust me!

It evaporates any aging concern right then and there, we immediately feel in our prime again, the cell memory puts us right back to the times when we felt truly beautiful. Instant vitality returns so powerfully that we like to celebrate, go to a party, have a drink with friends and enjoy this self-esteem high. How magical it feels to be seen, acknowledged and adored. I have witnessed and experienced it over and over again. After their face and body rejuvenating sessions with me, my clients are ready to show themselves to the world.

They say again and again that they feel and look 5-10 years younger.

Not so long ago, I struggled being the "happy wife." I tried hard to hide my real feelings and thoughts. I successfully concealed my permanent state of low energy from the many women who looked forward to seeing me. For many of my clients it was the highlight of their month. They were recharging and rejuvenating their bodies and faces with me and I had to be "on" for them. In my early fifties I had accepted the fact that half of my time here on earth had already past. I turned to eating whatever came to mind, thinking that I deserved to reward myself. My dress size jumped dramatically from 8 to 14. I just didn't care. My self worth was at an all time low. It took a doctor's diagnosis of a serious potential illness to shake me out of my downward spiral. Instead of giving me drugs to numb my emotional pain he insisted that I examine what the root cause of my physical condition was and change it immediately. I knew he was right, so I set out to change my life situation by taking a leap of faith. This was extremely challenging for me emotionally.

I am now on a mission to educate, inspire and empower my fellow sisters, especially members of my boomer generation. I call you to trust your inner strength, the power you are born with. Realize that it is in your own hands to determine how well and long you can live.

As I transformed, so did my life. A new dimension of the divine life force and powerful inspirations of great spiritual masters opened my heart and soul. This helped me recognize the miracle of being here and the significance of the divine purpose we are sent to fulfill. I encourage you to be creatively selfish for a time. Put yourself first. Be the most important person in your life. Practice self-love and self-worth and never allow anyone to manipulate you. Become a happy, healthy, magnet of light. People will flock around you and reflect your invigorating energy back to you in abundance.

> *"Your skin is the finest clothing but, of course, society demands something more than this."*
> ~ Mark Twain

THE FINEST CLOTHING

In mastering the art of skin care which began in my early 20's, I could not agree more with Mark Twain's assertion that our skin is the finest clothing. Our skin wraps us from head to toe in a treasure of living, intelligent and expressive tissues. Discovering the nature of our skin and the many approaches to skin care began for me in the schools and laboratories of Europe, and continues today in my studio in Northern California. Having helped tens of thousands of women look and feel better over the past 40 years, I want to share with you some of my discoveries and practices. I have many insights about the attention and care this *finest of clothing* needs to stay at its best. I feel that any and all efforts put toward regenerating and nourishing your skin is well worth the time, energy and investment. It is never too late to upgrade the care you bring to your receptive and intelligent skin. It renews itself at an astonishing rate and responds quickly to changes in nutrition. When the simple sequences of cleansing, nourishing and protecting are practiced, remarkable transformations are possible.

Most women know there are sets of rules to follow to maintain healthy skin. Obviously there is so much information regarding skincare tips and practices. Plentiful articles and recommendations are available and I want to support you by creating - *your list* - a regimen you enjoy implementing daily because the rewards to look and feel absolutely gorgeous is a worthwhile effort.

Here are just a few fundamental recommendations you integrate into your existing routine

1. Pay close attention to the amount of water you drink. (8 eight-ounce glasses per day)
2. Never skip cleansing before bedtime; that effort will maintain your youthfulness for years to come
3. Use good quality toners, serums and moisturizers that include Vitamin A and antioxidants to prevent dead skin cell build up between treatments and disarming free radicals.

Your skin is as unique as you are and accordingly is its need for optimal maintenance. Trust your skin in experienced expert hands to have a custom designed treatment protocol that rewards you with an ageless glowing complexion worth your investment.

Chapter 10

SOME FINAL
THOUGHTS

I am often asked what my day is like or whether I have a specific regimen that I follow. I feel as if the question they are really asking me is, "Is there something you are doing that is different or unique from my daily activities? Are you looking and feeling the way you do because of some esoteric breathing practice or a secret juice concoction that you have discovered or invented?" Even though I am German and prone to precise discipline, I can assure you my days are far from pressurized "to do" lists. They flow intuitively in a gentle manner most of the time. So here is a summary of a pretty typical day for me. I include it here to both dispel the possible rumors of a secret underground gym and to inspire you to live in a way that suits your joy and resourcefulness.

When I open my eyes in the morning, I relish for a moment the fact that I woke up, as in, at all. I have been gifted with yet another day on this miraculous earth. That sets in motion the tone in my heart and soul of deep gratitude. I am then holding, in my inner eye, my body from head to toe, thanking it for carrying me throughout my lifetime, never failing me. This is a loving scan and a way to get in touch with any blocks in my energy that may need extra attention. From there, I am moving on to consider the optimum nourishment it may need to support its efforts to keep me healthy and strong, as well as to fight off any disease that might diminish the quality of my life. I then "listen in" as my body responds clearly to the appreciation I show it. I sense it boosting a joyous energy that accompanies me throughout my day. My clients literally bathe in that healing energy and are surprised that their headaches disappear, chest pains subside and sadness vanishes.

MORNING MEDITATION

I enjoy lighting candles, burning some incense, opening my arms wide and inviting my spirit guides to join me. And they do. I can sense their presence all around me most mornings. I feel in loving company and relish this time, dwelling in those moments of just "being."

I have a new morning ritual now. I take 30-45 minutes to read, research and educate myself about the newest findings and discoveries in ageless living technologies. I am then preparing to engage with the wonderful women coming under my wings that day to help them feel and look gorgeous, nurture their soul and improve their health. So much joy to look forward to and I can't wait to arrive at my beautiful office, a sanctuary like no other.

MORNING NOURISHMENT

I enjoy drinking a glass of water with fresh lemon to alkalize my blood pH before anything else. I then start my exercise routine by running in the yard, stretching and jumping one hundred times on my rebounder. (It has to be a special soft bouncing design, so that you don't hurt the cushioning of your vertebrae). This takes usually 45 minutes, and there are no words to describe the joyful energy I feel afterwards. Over two decades ago I discovered rebounding exercise. I was surprised how different I felt when using it then. A year later, we remodeled our home and my Rebounder was forgotten in the basement. When I divorced three years ago I discovered it again and started to jump daily. One hundred jumps in the morning was part of my exercise routine. I had no more aches anywhere in my body and I attributed that to the intense cellular cleansing. The instant aerobic movement helped to flush waste from my cells. Anyone unable to move their body regularly and with flexibility has a high level of toxicity, which poisons the cells in the vital organs. Aside from insufficient nutrition, the primary cause of fatigue, disease, cell degeneration and premature aging is poor circulation to and from the tissues of your body. Your living cells and organs, when continually supplied with quality nutrients and oxygen will thrive only so long as toxic waste substances are concurrently removed and regularly excreted from your body. That is the primary duty of your lymphatic system. Rebounding aerobics effectively moves and recycles the lymph and the entire blood supply through the circulatory system many times during one session. This begins cellular cleansing instantly. Not every Rebounder on the market is beneficial. It has to be medium soft, so as to place no stress onto the cushioning around and between your joints, specifically on the discs of your vertebrae.

There is now no difference in my energy from the time I was in my early thirties to this day. This is true, even though I broke my back twice and healed perfectly without any traditional medical intervention. I used a German electromagnetic pulse device after it happened for the second time, which contributed to my fast recovery considerably. I continue to use it on a daily basis for the many benefits I feel it provides.

Please contact me for more information about this device. I call it my personal fountain of youth, keeping me healthy and vivacious.

I exfoliate my face and body every single day in the shower with a rough nylon strip for my body and a gentler exfoliating scrub for my face. Every other day I mask my face to keep the skin surface nourished, hydrated and moisturized. Vitamin Serum follows, and then a very emollient cream is applied to seal in all the ingredients the skin needs to maintain a perfect moisture level and regain a better elasticity. SPF of at least 35 on a daily basis follows before makeup application. Finishing up my morning beauty routine, I prepare my breakfast. I alternate between a veggies smoothie and a fruit smoothie, both made with protein powder, avocado, walnuts, and almond or coconut milk.

THE AFTERNOON

For lunch I mix together several spoons of almond butter and coconut oil. I love to use the delicious butter flavored coconut oil that John Roulac has created. He is the founder & CEO of Nutiva. At a gathering of friends recently he explained to me, how this unique combination of palm and coconut oil works to supplement dairy products. It was easy now to cut out butter. I confess to enjoying about 3 small cappuccinos a day, but I counteract this by taking mineral supplements.

THE EVENING DINNER

I love to have either chicken or fish once or twice a week. I never eat bread and I avoid most carbohydrates altogether. I refrain from sweets and eat raw cacao beans for the antioxidant benefits. I am very proud that I now can pass on chocolate or ice cream, I confess that I indulged in these before I adapted to my conscious eating habits. I check my water intake, to complete my daily quota. (There is my German precision. Exposed. I have a "water quota" and it feels perfectly normal to me.) Very empowering!

Ageless Tip
DESIGN YOUR
SLEEP

Go to sleep and wake up at the same time each day.

BED TIME

My evening beauty ritual looks like this. After thorough cleansing, I again exfoliate my face using a mild exfoliating acid twice a week, tone and apply a nighttime vitamin-rich skin cocktail. I finish my day with meditation, reviewing what the day presented to me and allowing space for my body to unwind and open my heart and mind to the fullness of being. I relax into receiving the "answers" to questions I had asked during the day. People I had thought about earlier in the day often have sent e-mails or have left messages for me. These confirm, in endless ways, that I am magically connected to this world and inspire me to learn more and continue mastering the art of ageless energy with its loving, connecting qualities. I am committed to grow into the most powerful and aligned human being I am meant to be. Moving away from confining beliefs and isolating realities, I am moving on to lay a new foundation to rise up on. One that will support a culture of abundance, love and vitality. Here at last I can thrive, day after day, in new and unexpected ways.

SOME THOUGHTS ABOUT THE MIND/BODY

I do everything to the best of my knowledge to keep my body in excellent health. I hope you do as well. You may want to pay close attention to its needs and learn about the requirements of its optimum service to you. As I mentioned earlier, your miraculous and precious body is the home of your soul and the vehicle that carries you through life. Make it of the utmost importance to nurture and keep it healthy, so it will never let you down, but will enable you to successfully follow your dreams and desires. Why would you risk weakening or even destroying the very entity that makes or breaks your dreams? If compromised, it could prevent you from achieving the mission you were sent here to complete.

You are a star in the universe - equipped with far more gifts and powers than you can comprehend. That is one of the reasons I encourage an active exploration into the deep layers of your soul. In doing so you have an opportunity to uncover the mysteries of your existence. I am still a novice at it. And yet my expanded horizons of understanding, my emotional transformations, the automatic youthful reversal of my body shape and the erasing of years from my face, inspire me to share these miraculous changes with you. My wish in doing so is to invite you to experience this magnitude of change for yourself, so that you might shift into a different worldview and elevate yourself into a blissful and soulful existence. I am inspired by what Dr. John Demartini has written in his book, *The Values Factor*, "You are here to raise your standards for yourself and to stretch yourself beyond your previous limits. You are here to inspire other to do the same so that humanity can break through any stagnant ways previous generations followed and catapult forward to newer and ever more magnificent ways of being, doing, and having."

You are here to transform not just yourself but others who are transforming with you. The aging ways that previous generations followed are indeed stagnant. The changes called for are changes in our being, changes in our actions and changes in what we have. Ageless ways open human hearts to live magnificently and courageously. Life will stop being measured in years and will measured by the evolving standards you are setting for yourself. Each year will be stretching the limits of the previous year.

It is my heart's sincere desire to meet you, see you,
look into your eyes one day. I hope to hear from you.
Perhaps in some way this book challenged you, inspired you,
and supported you to find your own springs of ageless
energy. I would be the happiest soul on this earth if that has
happened for you. To meet in person and attend one of my
Academy Workshops please visit the events section on my
website. www.agelessthebook.com/events.

Chapter 11

AGELESS LIVING AFFIRMATIONS

"Beliefs have the power to create and the power to destroy. Human beings have the awesome ability to take any experience of their lives and create a meaning that disempowers them or one that can literally save their lives."
~ Tony Robbins

Affirmations are a powerful tool to bring new perspectives to life. Spoken out loud, our bodies experience them as commands. These commands send out new information throughout our body/mind and frees up energy to flow without confusion and conflict. If you feel conflict arise, that is a signal to go in and question why it is there and listen to the information coming up.

Your beliefs become your thoughts,

Your thoughts become your words,

Your words become your actions,

Your actions become your habits,

Your habits become your values,

Your values become your destiny.

~ Mahatma Gandhi

AGELESS AFFIRMATIONS

The following set of 36 affirmations bring together Mahatma Gandhi's insightful sequence of the 6 elements shaping our destiny with the 6 elements of self-actualization. These are self-acceptance, personal growth, purpose in life, positive relationships, environmental mastery and autonomy.

The 36 affirmations are a powerful tool bringing your participation in life into alignment with your belief to live agelessly. Reciting them out loud helps bring a new clarity and power to areas you may need support in. In Gandhi's statement there is a progression in his sequence. Each aspect of your participation in life contributes to shaping the next expression, which ultimately consists of the shaping of your destiny. I trust these affirmations strengthen your resolve to live vibrantly in a world of limitless potential and ageless vitality. A recitation ritual in which you speak all thirty 36 will awaken a rich understanding of how these work together to weave your destiny.

AGELESS LIVING BELIEFS

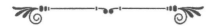

SELF-ACCEPTANCE

I am worthy of acceptance. My self-acceptance grows and matures each day. I accept all that I am and welcome all of my past and present. My beliefs align with the deepening and expansion of my self-acceptance. I live in a loving universe that accepts me as one of it's treasures.

PERSONAL GROWTH

I am worthy of growing in new and healthy ways, free of conflict. My personal growth mature each day. I grow steadily on my own and in groups. I grow in a universe that is intelligent and supportive.

PURPOSE IN LIFE

My purpose in life is clear and I through it I guide my life decisions. I accept my purpose in life. I trust my ability to align and act on my purpose. I live in a world of purpose and infinite intelligence.

POSITIVE RELATIONS WITH OTHERS

My relations with others are positive and supportive. I am enough and all who I meet are enough. I am worthy of harmonious, loving and supportive relations with all the people in my life. My positive relationships align with the deepening and expansion of my life journey.

ENVIRONMENTAL MASTERY

My environment is aligned with my abilities to master the elements needed to support my life in a joyful way. I am worthy and capable of living in my environment with mastery. I commit to master the needs of my physical environment. I live in a world of limitless possibilities.

AUTONOMY

My autonomy supports my life. I have the courage and clarity to be autonomous. I trust my own decisions and my abilities to determine for myself the path of my life. I am free from conflicts in my choices and value the advice of others. I live in a universe that supports my dreams and the dreams of all.

THOUGHTS ARISING FROM BELIEFS

SELF-ACCEPTANCE

My loving thoughts of acceptance open the understanding of my own self-worth. All my thoughts are welcome - all thoughts past and present. My thoughts align perfectly and effortlessly with my chosen beliefs and foster the deepening and expansion of my self-acceptance.

PERSONAL GROWTH

My thoughts of growing in new and healthy ways are free of conflict and align with my chosen beliefs. My thoughts are positive and align perfectly with my growth on my own and in groups.

PURPOSE IN LIFE

My thoughts are purposeful in my life. I align my thinking to my goals and aspirations. I trust my ability to cultivate a clear mind and to think with purpose. My thoughts align with my freely chosen beliefs about my purpose.

POSITIVE RELATIONS WITH OTHERS

My thoughts are supporting positive and harmonious relations. I am responsible for my thoughts. I commit to have and share thoughts of support for myself and others. Love inspires my thinking and clarity illuminates my mind. All my thoughts concerning my relations with others align effortlessly with my chosen beliefs.

ENVIRONMENTAL MASTERY

My thoughts support my capabilities to live and thrive in my environment with mastery. I commit to expand my intellect with new ideas, language and powers of persuasion to bring and sustain joy in my environment.

AUTONOMY

My thinking is supporting my own decisions and abilities to determine the path of my life. I am free from conflicts in my thinking and value the advice of others. My thoughts align perfectly with my freely chosen beliefs.

WORDS ARISING FROM THOUGHTS

SELF-ACCEPTANCE

My loving words of acceptance open the doors of ever deeper understanding of my personal worth. All my words are welcome, all my words past and present are accepted. My words align with the deepening and expansion of my self-acceptance.

PERSONAL GROWTH

My words, spoken to support my growing in new and healthy ways, are free of conflict and aligned with my chosen beliefs. My words are kind, positive and in alignment with my growth. My speech attracts to me all I need to thrive in a world of limitless possibilities.

PURPOSE IN LIFE

My words and speech are purposeful in my life. I align my words to support my goals and aspirations. I trust my ability to cultivate a clear mind and to speak with purpose. My words align with my freely chosen beliefs.

POSITIVE RELATIONS WITH OTHERS

My words weave positive and harmonious relations with others. I alone am responsible for my words. I commit to have and share words of support for myself and others. My words are inspired with loving kindness. My words align with my chosen beliefs about my relations with others in my life.

ENVIRONMENTAL MASTERY

My words support my capabilities to live and thrive in my environment with mastery. I am committed to expand my vocabulary with new ideas, language and powers of persuasion to bring and sustain joy in my environment.

AUTONOMY

My words, both spoken and written, support my own decisions and abilities to determine the path of my life. I am free from conflicts in my words and value the advice of others. My words align with my freely chosen belief that confirms the value of my autonomy in an intelligent and loving universe.

ACTIONS ARISING FROM WORDS

SELF-ACCEPTANCE

My actions support the acceptance of my life. I accept all I am through my aligned actions. My actions align with the deepening and expansion of my self-acceptance. I act in alignment with my chosen belief that I am worthy of complete acceptance in a loving universe.

PERSONAL GROWTH

My actions are in alignment with growing in new and healthy ways, free of conflict. My actions are supporting my steady growth on my own and in groups. I trust my ability to act on my decisions to grow. My actions align with my freely chosen beliefs about my goals and abilities to blossom in a universe of infinite powers.

PURPOSE IN LIFE

My actions are aligned with my purpose in this life. I trust my ability to act and move into ever greater alignment with my purpose. My actions align with my freely chosen beliefs about my purpose in a meaningful universe.

POSITIVE RELATIONS WITH OTHERS

My actions bring clarity, safety and loving qualities to all my relationships. My actions align with my freely chosen beliefs about my relationships in a loving universe.

ENVIRONMENTAL MASTERY

My actions are aligned with living in my environment with mastery. I act in a committed way to master the needs of my physical environment. My actions align perfectly with my freely chosen beliefs about life in a supportive and abundant universe.

AUTONOMY

My actions are aligned with own decisions and my abilities to determine for myself the path of my life. I act free from conflicts in my choices to act and value the advice of others. My actions align uniquely with my freely chosen beliefs about my freedom in an infinitely creative universe.

HABITS ARISING FROM ACTION

SELF-ACCEPTANCE

My habits are supporting the acceptance of my life . I accept all I am through my aligned habits. My habits of acceptance grow with my life journey. My habits align with the deepening and expansion of my self-acceptance.

PERSONAL GROWTH

My habits align with my growth and evolution in ever new and healthy ways, free of conflict. My habits are a solid foundation, supporting me steadily on my own path of growth and in my enrichment in groups. I trust my habits to support my decisions to change and grow. My habits align with my freely chosen beliefs about my growth in a creative universe.

PURPOSE IN LIFE

My habits are aligned with my purpose in this life. I trust my ability to free myself from habits that no longer serve me and replace them with habits that are in ever greater alignment with my freely chosen beliefs about my purpose.

POSITIVE RELATIONS WITH OTHERS

My habits bring clarity, safety and loving qualities to all my relationships. My habits support the freely chosen beliefs I hold regarding my relationships in a universe of limitless love.

ENVIRONMENTAL MASTERY

My habits are aligned with living in my environment with mastery. I act in a committed way, utilizing my good habits to master the needs of my physical environment. My habits support the freely chosen beliefs I hold regarding the mastery of my environment in a universe of limitless abundance.

AUTONOMY

My habits are aligned with own decisions and my abilities to determine, for myself, the path of my life. I am free from habits that are in conflict with my choices and decisions. My habits support the consciously chosen beliefs I hold regarding my autonomy in a universe of limitless freedom.

VALUES ARISING FROM HABITS

SELF-ACCEPTANCE

My values support the acceptance of my life through all its twists and turns. I accept all I am through my aligned values. My values align perfectly and clearly with the deepening and expansion of my own self-acceptance. My values align with my freely chosen beliefs of my own worth.

PERSONAL GROWTH

My values align with and support my growing in new and healthy ways. My values are free from conflict of any kind. My values support me and form a foundation of which my steady growth advances on my own and in groups. I trust my ability to value my decisions to grow in alignment with my freely chosen beliefs.

PURPOSE IN LIFE

My values are aligned with my purpose in this life. I trust my ability to sustain and refine my values in ever greater alignment with my purpose. I am energized by my values that are in perfect alignment with my freely chosen beliefs about my purpose in a world of infinitely expanding richness.

POSITIVE RELATIONS WITH OTHERS

My values support and inform the clarity, safety and loving qualities I have in all my relationships. I am fortified by my values. My highest values are in perfect alignment with my freely chosen beliefs about my relationships in a world of infinite love and support.

ENVIRONMENTAL MASTERY

My values are aligned with living in my environment with mastery. I act in a committed way to master the needs of my physical environment. I am strengthened by my values. These are in perfect alignment with my freely chosen beliefs about my environment in a world of limitless abundance.

AUTONOMY

My values are aligned perfectly with my autonomy. I value my own decisions and my abilities to determine, for myself, the path of my life. I value confidently, free from conflicts in my choices and value the advice of others. I am enriched by my values. These are in effortless alignment with my freely chosen beliefs about my freedom in a world of limitless joy and possibilities.

DESTINY ARISING FROM VALUES

SELF-ACCEPTANCE

My destiny is felt and welcomed in my life . I accept all that is destined for me and accept all I have contributed to the shaping of my destiny. My destiny is in perfect alignment with my freely chosen beliefs concerning my own self-acceptance in a world of infinite love.

PERSONAL GROWTH

My destiny is unfolding in alignment with my goals and feel free of conflict. My destiny is supporting my growth and my growth in groups. I trust my ability to allow my destiny to be refined and reconfigured through my participation in life.

PURPOSE IN LIFE

My destiny is perfectly aligned with my purpose in this life. I trust my destiny to unfold and move into ever greater alignment with my purpose and be influenced by my participation in my life.. My destiny is in alignment with my freely chosen beliefs regarding my purpose in a meaningful universe of infinite possibilities.

POSITIVE RELATIONS WITH OTHERS

My destiny is unfolding in clarity, safety and loving-kindness in all my relationships. I accept that my participation in my life is refining and reconfiguring my destiny around my relations. My destiny is in perfect alignment with my beliefs about my positive relations in a world of limitless support and love.

ENVIRONMENTAL MASTERY

My destiny is to live in my environment with mastery. I accept that my participation in my life is refining and reconfiguring my destiny. My destiny is in perfect alignment with my beliefs about my environmental mastery in a world of limitless support, creativity and love.

AUTONOMY

My destiny radiates integrity with my own decisions. My destiny is to live forever free from allowing others to determine the direction of my life for me. I accept that I am free to participate in my life in ways that refine and reconfigure my destiny. My destiny is in perfect alignment with my freely chosen beliefs about my own autonomy. I thrive in a universe that celebrates and supports the free will of the magnificent and mysterious being that I am.

ABOUT THE AUTHOR

Hedda Adler is a speaker, author, trainer, coach and skin care expert. She is expanding and deepening the idea of longevity and exposing the deficiencies of our current "aging beliefs." She is a recipient of the C.I.D.E.S.C.O.* Diplomat Certification Award; the world's most prestigious International Certification Award in Aesthetics. Hedda mastered the arts of Skin Care, Health and Wellness in her home country of Germany, as well as in France, Italy, Austria and Switzerland. She has attracted a large and loyal following throughout her 40 years of practice, supporting tens of thousands of women worldwide not only to look and feel their best, but to mentally and physically turn back "the aging clock." Hedda is a leader in the increasingly significant shift in beliefs and attitudes that she calls "The Ageless Living Revolution." She is the founder of the large MeetUp group, Courageous Women in Transition: A Miraculous Life At Any Age. Hedda is a mother and grandmother and is currently residing in the San Francisco Bay Area of California. www.heddaadler.com

*Comité International d'Esthétique et de Cosmétologie

For Ageless Workshops and Event information:

www.AgelesstheBook.com/events

To book Hedda Adler for speaking engagements:

www.HeddaAdler.com/speaking

To contact Hedda Adler:

www.HeddaAdler.com/contact

Email: hedda@heddaadler.com

Made in the USA
Middletown, DE
22 January 2017